ARMAGEDDON'S WALLS

ARMAGEDDON'S WALLS

British Pill Boxes and Bunkers
1914–1918

Peter Oldham

Pen & Sword
MILITARY

First published in Great Britain in 2014 by
PEN AND SWORD MILITARY
an imprint of
Pen and Sword Books Ltd
47 Church Street
Barnsley
South Yorkshire S70 2AS

Copyright © Peter Oldham, 2014

ISBN 978 1 78303 300 3

Printed and bound in England
by CPI Group (UK) Ltd, Croydon, CR0 4YY

Typeset in Times New Roman by
CHIC GRAPHICS

Pen & Sword Books Ltd incorporates the imprints of
Pen & Sword Archaeology, Atlas, Aviation, Battleground, Discovery,
Family History, History, Maritime, Military, Naval, Politics, Railways,
Select, Social History, Transport, True Crime, and Claymore Press,
Frontline Books, Leo Cooper, Praetorian Press, Remember When,
Seaforth Publishing and Wharncliffe.

For a complete list of Pen and Sword titles please contact
Pen and Sword Books Limited
47 Church Street, Barnsley, South Yorkshire, S70 2AS, England
E-mail: enquiries@pen-and-sword.co.uk
Website: www.pen-and-sword.co.uk

Contents

Introduction

The British Army and her Commonwealth Allies went to war in 1914 with little knowledge and experience of constructing permanent, shell-proof protective structures. Some masonry fortifications, such as defensive blockhouses in South Africa, had been built but the Royal Engineers of the Army were more versed in simple temporary defences suitable for mobile warfare. Training was in the rapid erection of protection which was presumed to be for a limited period, and the layout of wire obstacles, trenches, demolitions and bridging as laid out in the official Manual of Field Engineering which had been published in 1911 and reprinted in 1914 due to the rapid expansion of the Army.[1] This manual gave much advice on cover for observation posts, artillery and machine guns, all based on simple overhead cover as protection from splinters. This lack of preparedness was acknowledged by the Royal Engineers after the war when the corps history recorded:

> 'The regulations and the training before the war only envisaged the use of field defences for purely temporary purposes, and especially emphasised the necessity for the resumption of an energetic advance at the earliest moment. The conception that energetic advance might prove impossible and that the operations might degenerate into the conditions of siege warfare had not apparently entered the minds of those responsible for army training.'[2]

Home defences were a limited number of forts around naval ports and Martello towers on the east coast. It was considered that the Navy was quite able to defend Britain's coasts. The army establishment did include some fortress engineers but these were trained and equipped for coastal defence and electrical works such as searchlights.

The Germans on the other hand, as with the other continental countries such as France, Belgium, Italy, Holland, Poland and Austria, had been constantly renewing and updating border forts for several centuries. They had also maintained fortification and siege elements of their armies who were experienced in designing and constructing strong shelters. Both German and

INTRODUCTION

French armies began the war with a degree of expertise in what was to become a static war with little movement. Both were also quicker than the British to start building shell-proof shelters for machine guns, artillery, command centres, aid posts etc.

However, from a stationary starting point, by 1918 the British were to surpass both enemy and friends in the design and construction, with supply and logistics, of such shell-proof cover for troops and defensive positions. A number of systems and standard designs, for both cast-in-place and pre-cast concrete, were devised and established using technical advances and innovations based on the previous three years' experiences.

This book gives the history of development and innovation of concrete bunkers, pill boxes, blockhouses and general concrete constructions during the First World War. Many of these structures – some showing obvious signs of war damage – still exist in France and Belgium today, although the number is dwindling due to constant land reclamation for agriculture, housing, factory sites and roads in the inevitable progress of economy and populations. The work dwells minimally on technicalities of concrete, construction and design.

All the existing structures, with photographs (except for some which are impractical because of dense vegetation), are shown on the following pages. Many entries have contemporary maps showing how they fitted into a defensive system, whilst for others the location can be identified from the text. GPS coordinates are given for each entry except for a few which are on private land and where privacy has been requested. For all the other entries, some are in public areas but many are on private land and visitors should respect owners' rights.

It may be that, tucked away in a farmer's barn or wood somewhere, there exists a pill box or bunker not listed in this book. There are certainly quite a number of fortified or strengthened cellars of houses and buildings which either still stand or were rebuilt on the same site (an example is the walls and roof of the cellar of the bakery at 179 Dikkebusseweg, Ypres, which comprises thick concrete and steel beams). However, all of the types, patterns and systems which were designed or evolved are covered with examples and, where known, any historical facts pertaining to the structure.

In many cases it is possible to determine who constructed and who used the existing vestiges: some engineers and occupants left good records of their involvement. Sometimes little or no information is available, although occasionally it can be deduced, and the reader will find many such examples marked as 'probably or possibly by...'. A number of constructions do not appear in records and are evident only by their continuing existence, being large monoliths by persons and units unknown, often showing signs of severe actions such as shellfire, found in fields and woods. Although anonymous, they do have a history of extraordinary events.

Apologies to the people of France and Belgium who find their town and village names misspelt. It is a fact that the British Army changed and anglicised many place names, it can also be difficult for a non-domicile to be aware of some modernisations of names, especially in Flemish Belgium. For example, it is found that St Eloi is nowadays St Elooi, Messines is Mesen and Ypres is properly Ieper. On a smaller scale, Langhof Farm is Lankhof Farm, and La Signy Farm is named both Ferme de Lassigny and la Signy Fme on different official French maps. It is hoped that these errors and changes do not cause any confusion to the reader.

Author's note
During the progress of this work several of the structures recorded have been demolished and these are noted in the text. This has continued up until the time shortly before publication, when evidence of other, more recent, demolitions is found; for example Tuff's Farm, near Ypres, was cleared to make space for farm buildings and Gauche Wood, near Cambrai, as part of land clearance and neither exists now. More recently, August 2013, the large triple bunker at Hoograaf, B24, has been demolished. Many structures have been listed and protected by local authorities, however the continuing loss of many confirms the need to record what is left.

P.C.O. 29 January 2014

Acknowledgements

I would like to thank those who have provided help in various ways: Pierre Capelle, who has an unsurpassed knowledge of the Cambrai and Somme areas; Hannelore Decoodt, compiling the Inventaris for Flanders (www.onroerenderf goed.be), who has been very helpful and loaned some photographs; Aurel Sercu and his local knowledge of Boezinge; Bob Findley; Jeremy Banning, Dr Frank Andrews of Sandwich; Emmanuel Bril, who has a wide and extensive knowledge of the Hazebrouck area; Simon Jones; Keith Knight, Eddy Lambrecht; Iain McHenry; Rino Delcombe, a good Ypres photographer who improved on some of my photographs; the staff of Saffron Walden public library and the National Archives.

CHAPTER 1

Development

Contrary to some earlier printed statements by military historians, the British did not 'discover' concrete pill boxes first in the summer of 1917.

The first recorded British concrete machine gun post or concrete dugout or emplacement (the term 'pill box' had yet to appear two years later) was in August 1915, although the 2nd Royal Anglesey Royal Engineers recorded – with little detail – completing experimental dugouts at Ypres in May 1915, and later having to stop work because of a lack of cement. The 1st London Field Company Royal Engineers (later re-designated 509th Field Company RE) began making concrete dug-outs for machine gun crews on August 1st around Wilson's Farm, St Jean. They then constructed several more during the winter of 1915/16. The 1/2nd West Riding Field Company (later 57th Field Company) on 14 August 1915 built a machine gun post with concrete protection for the crew at Chateau des Trois Tours near Ypres. This still exists in the private wood surrounding the chateau. The 7th Field Company, constructing a defence line near Elverdinge in August 1915, worked on 'some concrete machine gun emplacements made as experiments'. Britain's allies were also quick off the mark. The Canadian Overseas Railway Construction Corps arrived at Fortem, near Ramskapelle, in August 1915 and began '*construction of Materials Yard and making m.g. emplacements (concrete) and observation tower*'. They also helped the Belgian Army on concrete constructions near the front line before being returned to Southampton in September 1915.

Other experimental work and trials were carried on elsewhere: on 12 September 1915 the General Officer Commanding and Commander Royal Engineers of 50th (Northumbrian) Division went to Mont Noir (Kemmel) to see the results of shooting 18pdr shells against various types of reinforced concrete work.

At the northern end of the line near Boezinge, where ground water meant that trenches were often raised behind breastwork sand bags and butts, 62nd Field Company recorded in February 1916:

'Two new MG emplacements constructed off Fargate, one north of Wyatt's Lane, one south of Wellgate. Covered communication trench to each. Each emplacement made about 6'x6' – heavy frames – two rows of steel girders opposite ways set in concrete. Loophole with girders and concrete above.'

Such early works were not confined to the Ypres salient. Second Lieutenant Case was killed on 14 August 1915 whilst working on concrete machine gun emplacements at Trench 80, Armentières. The 7th Field Company REs were still building concrete machine gun emplacements at

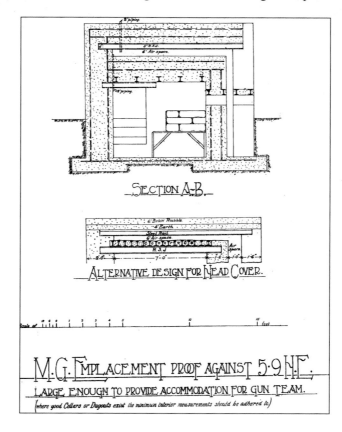

SECTION A-B.

ALTERNATIVE DESIGN FOR HEAD COVER.

M.G. EMPLACEMENT PROOF AGAINST 5.9 H.E.

LARGE ENOUGH TO PROVIDE ACCOMMODATION FOR GUN TEAM.

(where good Cellars or Dugouts exist the minimum interior measurements should be adhered to)

DEVELOPMENT

Armentières in October 1915. At Festubert in November, where trenches were difficult because of the low lying and wet land, 12th Divisional Engineers constructed concrete shelters strong enough to withstand 15cm shells. The engineers recorded the design of the machine gun posts – which incorporated 6in air space in the roof to reduce concussion – made in 1915 at Festubert, as shown in the diagram, left.

Several attempts at producing an air space as shown in the drawing were made but it was found to be difficult in field conditions. An example of a construction to the design existed in Festubert, shown above, until demolished in recent years.

Further south on the Somme early concrete machine gun emplacements, of the type later to be called pill boxes, had also been constructed. Handing-over notes from the 151st Field Company Royal Engineers (38th Division) to the 83rd (20th Division) on 26 July 1916 listed all machine gun emplacements on the front of Beaumont Hamel-Hébuterne. At La Signy Farm opposite Serre they had constructed four, reported as *'Concrete emplacement. Table Mounting'*.

Not all British constructions were by the Royal Engineers. The Australian, New Zealand and Canadian engineers, and later the Americans, were all active in this field and much of what remains today is the result of their endeavours.

Additionally, not all concrete work was carried out by engineers. The artillery did much construction work to house and protect artillery pieces and

3

crews and to provide safety for observers in artillery observation posts. Some Corps Heavy Artillery headquarters had Royal Engineer officers attached to give advice and guidance. Machine gunners also provided protection to gun crews, such as 27th Brigade MGC who spent much of January to March 1916 constructing concrete emplacements in and around Ploegsteert Wood. They made their own, of steel rails and concrete, as the attached REs were busy with other defence works as well as protection for the machine guns.

Other MG companies influenced the siting and design of emplacements. Some work was also carried out by engineers before setting off for France and Belgium. While based at Imber on Salisbury Plain in the winter of 1916/17, the 502 (Wessex) Field Company RE, which was shortly to set off for the front, practised building concrete shelters and recorded:

'Our work was the construction, above gun pits and dug-outs, of shell-proof cover, composed of strata of concrete, chalk and earth, with 'air spaces' in between; the positions were afterwards shelled by 9.2in howitzers with a view to testing the accuracy of the guns and the strength of the cover we had made.'[3]

All such constructions were described variously as concrete machine gun emplacements, concrete dugouts, blockhouses or shell-proof shelters as no collective name had been coined. Terms were either from the Boer War, such as blockhouse, or a simple description such as MGE. The term Mebu was sometimes later adopted, mainly by the infantry to describe and record their struggles; *mannschafts eisenbeton unterstände* (reinforced concrete man shelter or Mebu) had been found on captured German engineering documents.

The development of shell-proof protection for machine guns, troops, unit headquarters, medical posts etc found favour among many, however not all higher-echelon staff were enthusiastic. Some considered that the provision of such shelter engendered a defensive spirit at the expense of the offensive, and some thought the expenditure of manpower and materials unnecessary. The Commander Royal Engineers of 39th Division, Lieutenant Colonel Hopkins, commented in January 1917 on works carried out by Field Companies under his command:

'There has often been a great waste of labour and materials... protection with concrete against anything over 5'9" is not possible...any concrete work will not set hard enough in less than two months...the use of concrete as protection against smaller shells is not worth the labour...'

Many of the British shelters, especially in the early part of the war, were based on an inner lining of prefabricated steel sheets which were named elephant iron. The most frequently used was the standard English Large Elephant Steel Shelter, which sometimes became known as the Champagne shelter. This comprised three sheets per section, bolted together at 1/3rd points, as shown below, and gave an inner height of just over 6 feet. It also came in a smaller version which was designed to provide shelter for four men.

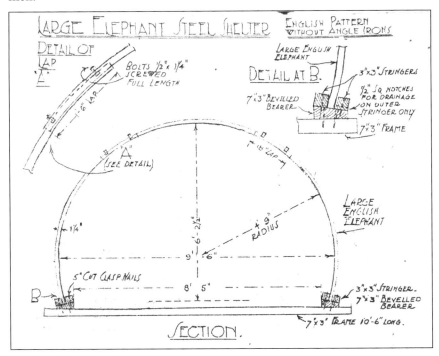

An alternative pattern, which was also used, comprised two sheets, with more pronounced corrugations, which were held together at the ceiling with a bolted steel rail. Some early specifications classified these as Elephant sheets, as opposed to English sheets for the finer corrugations, however the two descriptions have become blurred and mixed over time with the term Elephant Iron being used for most structures of this type. In many cases the

DEVELOPMENT

steel has rusted away, leaving the impression in the concrete. Examples of how these two steel sheet patterns appear today are shown to the left, the sheet overlap can be seen either 1/3 up the arc, or a steel beam overhead.

These shelters were almost always provided with external protection, which could vary from a thin layer of soil and stones to render it bullet and shrapnel proof, to several feet of reinforced concrete to make it heavy shell-proof. Sandbags were frequently used and could be in layers of several feet, as in the photo below.

For some early uses of such constructions it was presumed that a layer of unreinforced concrete would provide protection from heavy artillery shells, however this was found to be insufficient as in this example (next page) near Vlamertinghe, where almost complete collapse has occurred.

There are many similar constructions where steel reinforcement is evident in the concrete and damage has been limited.

The term 'pill box' first appears in print on the front page of *The Times*, on 2 August 1917, having been written on 1 August, describing the opening attack at Ypres on 31 July. The reporter, describing the ground fought over and the obstacles faced, wrote that:

> 'The favourite type of German stronghold is a structure of concrete made all in one piece, and not built of blocks, which has been named "the German pill-box". Used singly they are merely shelters or substitutes for dug-outs. With the proper internal arrangements and loopholes they are machine-gun posts, or clustered together they make redoubts. They are not easily destroyed by shell fire, but so terrific was our bombardment of the area attacked that these pill-boxes, where they were not shattered, were thrown upon their sides or left ridiculously standing on their roofs. Some are big enough to hold 20-30 men.'

It is not known how far forward the reporter went or how much he relied on the description by troops. From the report it can be deduced that he was at the northern part of the Salient, following troops from the Guards and 38th (Welsh) Divisions, from whom he probably learned of the term. As with most army slang the true and exact origin is difficult to identify but it can be determined that the term had been used before 31 July. Men of both divisions had experience of German machine gun posts before the attack began as many raids had taken place. The reports of these raids, such as by Lieutenant Mahomed and men of the 1st Scots Guards on 25 July to identify an emplacement across the canal, always referred to 'concrete dug outs' or 'concrete blockhouses' and battalion war diaries with reports of the attack repeat these names as the slang had not yet percolated from the ranks to the officers.

Apart from seeing the German concrete emplacements, troops of both these divisions had seen their own, and in many cases had been involved as working parties in building them. It is unlikely that a typical Tommy on a working party said he was working on a 'concrete machine gun emplacement'.

It is also unlikely that the slang term pill box (pill box, pillbox and pill-box have all been used, the writer has adopted the former as being more prevalent in later official British RE and infantry usage) emanates from the oft-perceived likeness to a medicine container. These medical pill boxes were generally round whereas the concrete 'pill box' was almost invariably square or rectangular. Round shaped ones were very few and far between until 1918, being rather more complicated and difficult to construct. *The Official History of the Great War* for 1917 (written in 1948, by which time the term was in general circulation) is also a little ambiguous. Describing the preparations for the Messines offensive in June 1917 and the expected and known German defences and troop shelters it states: *'In the distance they looked like, and were called, "pillboxes", and those loopholed strongpoints appeared as pillar-boxes.'*[4]

It is apparent that the embrasure was seen as being similar to a posting box. The name pillar box had been used long before the Ypres fighting in 1917. The war diary of 63rd Field Company RE, attached to 9th (Scottish) Division, recorded in their work schedule for March 1916 their work in progress around Ploegsteert Wood: *'Royal Artillery Observation Posts and MG emplacements, "Pillar Boxes" sites selected'*. This is probably the first written use of such a term for a structure. The Australians first used the term, as 'Pillar box', on 5 September 1917.[5] Although they had come up against concrete blockhouses at Messines in June, they had picked up the term while gaining intelligence and preparing for an attack on the Menin Road later in September. The preparations included plans for dislodging Germans from their strongholds, as recorded by the 2nd Field Company Australian Engineers on 17 September 1917:

'Charges of 10 slabs of guncotton are made up & these are to be employed in demolition of concrete dugouts known as "pill boxes" if any of these are encountered which hold out against infantry.'

Before long the term began to appear in battalion war diaries and was being officially adopted. Other terms were also used, the 8th Devons recorded action around both 'pepper boxes' and 'pill boxes' as being the same. Towards the later fighting in 1917 the word was in general usage although 'blockhouse' and 'dugout' remained in currency; 'shelter' also started to be more widely used, probably mainly due to the increase in aerial bombing and the need for overhead protection.

In 1918 the Americans described Langhof Farm as *'a machine gun nest'*, the Canadians had been using 'nest' for some time for their own machine gun positions, as had the Royal Engineers. The Australians also used the term occasionally: the 5th Infantry Brigade decided in March 1918 that *'certain pill boxes in the Brigade area should be converted into MG nests'*.

Although a commonly used word today, 'bunker', generally meaning a sub-ground shelter, was rarely if ever used during the Great War by either side. The word bunker had been used in English and probably other languages as a storage place for coal and fuel, however its military usage seems to originate with the Germans in their 1930s constructions. *'Abri'* was also used to a lesser degree for a shell-proof shelter, largely by those who had been closely affiliated with the French army and adopted some of their terms.

Not all of the pill boxes were built to house machine guns, in fact only a minority have embrasures; the majority are simply shelters from artillery or aerial bombs. Many were built specifically to provide protection for unit headquarters, communication and medical posts and for troops who were based at supply and storage dumps. Engineers of the Tramways and Foreways Companies who had the task of operating and maintaining the extensive light railways near the front – a target for German shells – often needed strong shelters, which was recognised and the REs stipulated that *'a dug-out should always be constructed near the terminus of all lines'*.[6]

Throughout 1916 various units of the Royal Engineers constructed concrete machine gun emplacements, shelters, dugouts and observation posts along the British sectors of the Western Front, mainly the northern parts, where the front was fairly static with no major offensives planned on the scale of further south on the Somme. The front between Arras and the Ypres salient was, apart from some small-scale attacks (perhaps not so small-scale for those involved, such as at The Bluff and St Eloi), generally fairly quiet

DEVELOPMENT

with no planned offensives and defences were strengthened against a possible German attack. These defences in in the Salient contained many concrete shell-proof emplacements and shelters. However they were generally the result of local initiatives by divisional troops, with little backing from higher echelons, and such works were interspersed with other engineer duties such as road maintenance, water supply, trenches and wiring.

One exception to this was the 6th (Siege) Company, Royal Monmouth Royal Engineers. One of the few companies to specialise in siege works and construction, and not being attached to a division which was liable to frequent movements, they spent most of their time in the Ypres salient in 1916 concreting for machine gun, artillery observation and command posts in the forward zones. One notable example was Red House observation post near St Jean which received and withstood a direct hit by a heavy shell. The resultant damage, which did not render the post unusable, was recorded in 1916.[7]

Early constructions, and the effect of shell fire on them, were later studied when the British adopted a defensive policy. This included the damage by controlled explosion, in a test in 1917, to a concrete machine gun emplacement which had been constructed at Kemmel in 1915. The drawing below shows the effect of the explosion; 10lbs (4.5kg) of guncotton was detonated and the resultant damage to the concrete and reinforcement

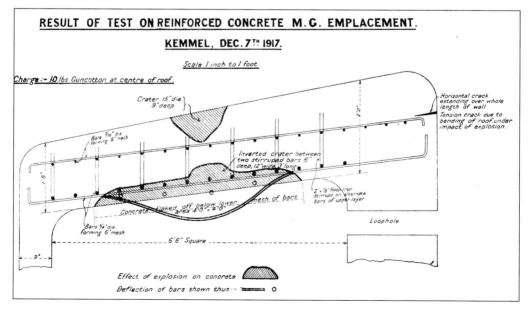

11

measured. Also measured was the amount of concrete flaking from the roof which would potentially harm any occupants. Recommendations were made regarding thickness of concrete and arrangement of reinforcing steel for future use, but these were not always practicable in field conditions.

The limiting of structural damage and protection to personnel inside had been considered by engineers and constructors, many of whom had the job of producing this in very difficult circumstances and with limited amounts and types of materials. It had been found however that many engineer officers had little or no knowledge of the function of reinforcement, and the Royal Engineers later reported:

> 'Excepting experts, who had been engaged in concrete in peace time, most officers had only a hazy notion of the principles of concrete or of its application to defence works; especially was there ignorance of the principles of reinforcement; and a number of works, faulty in design and unsuitable to their purpose, sprang up along the front. A very common fault was the use of too large a proportion of reinforcement. Girders or rails, indiscriminately buried in concrete, only served to break it up into layers, and, when struck by a shell, caused the whole mass to crack and disintegrate.'[8]

The photo detail of the roof of an artillery command shelter at Wieltje (B61) (top right), is a good example of the problem. It is a classic example of reinforcing metal separating the layers rather than strengthening the whole. It can be seen that the steel rails are forming laminated layers, and above that the smaller steel – in this case farm gates – forming another separating layer. Hence, the structure is weakened into three layers, rather than strengthened into a homogeneous mass.

The concept of an air space acting as a buffer which would take compressive forces, on detonation of a shell, between the exterior and an inner wall or roof, led to the common use of burster courses laid on the outside. This generally took the form of concrete blocks (although tree trunks or masonry rubble were also used in some circumstances, but with reduced effect). With a high demand for these, the Third Army set up a production factory at Anzin, producing concrete blocks 24 x 12 x 3 inches 'for use as burster layers for gun and machine gun pits' and some units set up smaller scale production units. The manner of their use, over an earth-covered shelter, can be seen in the bottom photograph on the right.

Engineering companies which manufactured their own burster blocks included the Australians; the 15th Field Company, based at Ypres Post Office in November 1917, made moulds for concrete slabs using a strong concrete mix although production was limited as before long their division was transferred elsewhere. Bursters were also manufactured close to point of usage and could be sized to accommodate the precise needs of the job in hand, as illustrated in the photograph on page 14 where an infantry working party, supervised by engineers, is stacking bursters which had been cast a day or two beforehand, to be used in the construction of a steel-lined concrete shelter near the front in the Ypres Salient in the spring of 1918.

Although the British had been constructing shell-proof shelters, observation posts, machine gun emplacements, command posts etc from mid 1915 through 1916 and 1917, these were generally the result of local unit

initiatives responding to local needs, such as the constructions in the Lys valley and around Festubert which were built because ground conditions with high water tables prevented the use of sub-ground dugouts for shelter. Not all troops – or their superiors – were enthusiastic about concrete shelters; the 75th Field Company RE, Guards Division, started work on a pill box at St Jean near Ypres in early 1916 before leaving the front to go into reserve. On returning to the front a month later they recorded:

> '13/5/16. MGE no. 8F carried on with. This concrete emplacement has not been completed since worked on by this Company when last in this sector.'

Only late in 1917 and into 1918 was there any large-scale planning for construction with supplies of previously unobtainable engineering materials being made available. Impetus had been given following the discovery of the large numbers and scale of German works. After the 1918 German spring offensive, when the line had been held and defences were bolstered as much as possible against further movement, the scale of construction operations mushroomed with high-level backing and planning for permanent fortifications.

The defences in 1918 were by now highly organised, utilising much experience gained from both defending and attacking, and studying and analysing German methods. Successive defence lines from the front-line systems with support and reserve lines under the control of a division, with Corps Lines and then Army Lines (often given colours as names, such as Purple Line and Brown Line) provided a successive and well-co-ordinated system of zones of responsibility. Lastly, in the rear there was the GHQ Line (not to be confused with GHQ Lines 1 and 2 which were the front and support lines south of Ypres in summer 1918). This ran from the south where it joined the French Army south of Amiens, to the north where between Poperinge and St Omer it joined with the Belgian Army. North of St Omer, in an arc past Watten and Dunkerque towards Veurne, the land was inundated to make it impassable.

The construction of pill boxes and shelters in the rear areas, often hitherto little affected by the war, often meant that dwellings, farmhouses and farm buildings were to be utilised. The arrangements then needed to cater for the fact that many were occupied by civilians and that trees sometimes needed to be cut down and crops destroyed to maintain views and field of fire. Army instructions were issued to ease the effects on the inhabitants. The Second Army issued a memo to Corps on 8 June 1918:

'With reference to your verbal enquiries on the subject of the construction of O.P., M.G. emplacements etc, for the West Hazebrouck Line, in houses which are still in occupation by the inhabitants, when you have made your reconnaissance and decided on the houses you require to use, we will take the question up with the French Mission in order to come to some arrangement with the inhabitants or have them evacuated.'

A few weeks later more instructions on this topic followed, with details of a firm policy. The instructions concluded:

'Subject to the general policy, the decision as to what houses should be destroyed is left to Corps Commanders.

In all cases lists of the houses that have been destroyed or damaged in accordance with these instructions should be forwarded to Army Headquarters for notification to the French or Belgian Missions, and to the Claims Commission.'

The GHQ Line was the last-ditch defence line: if this fell the war would effectively be over as there would only be a fighting retreat to protect the embarkation of forces at the Channel ports.

CHAPTER 2

The Somme to Arras

The GHQ Line in this sector ran to the west of Amiens. Vestiges of the line here, where it crossed the Somme, are a number of GHQ pattern pill boxes built to the standard specification with a few minor alterations. The GHQ specification gave full details of how the defences were to be sited, constructed and defended. The standard pill box was quite capable of withstanding a direct hit from a heavy artillery shell. It housed two Vickers machine guns which could be fired over the roof from platforms at the rear or from inside with an arc of fire of 60 degrees. The design included reinforced concrete tables for the guns.

The diagram shows the general shape and layout of the pill box, with two interior Vickers machine guns. A unique feature was the inclusion of several 6 inch diameter pipes for ventilation and the attachment of a steel pipe which ran for several hundred yards to the rear so that fresh air could be forced in. It was also intended that in the case of capture this pipe could be used to force poison gas into the chamber although this was never carried out. A wall thickness of 3 feet, with steel reinforcing bars, gave a good solidity and strength.

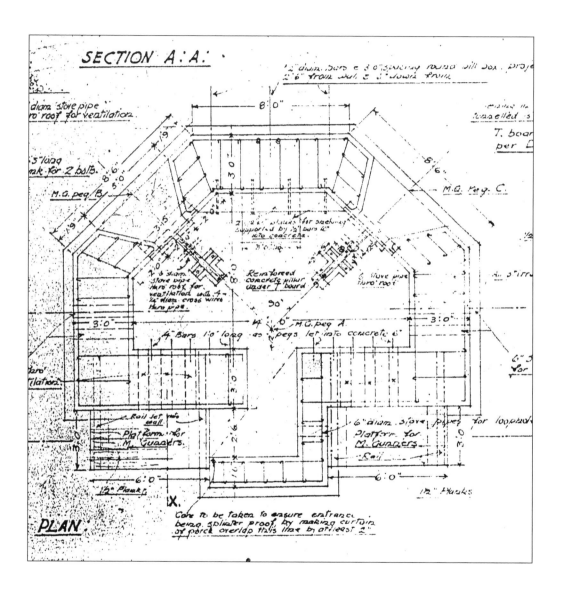

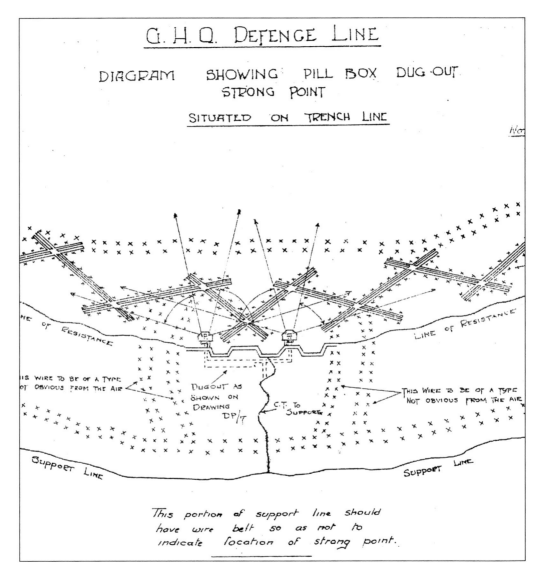

G. H. Q. DEFENCE LINE

DIAGRAM SHOWING PILL BOX DUG·OUT STRONG POINT

SITUATED ON TRENCH LINE

This portion of support line should have wire belt so as not to indicate location of strong point.

The specification also gave guidance on siting the pill boxes in pairs, for mutual protection, behind barbed wire and trenches, whilst accepting that ground and local conditions could vary this.

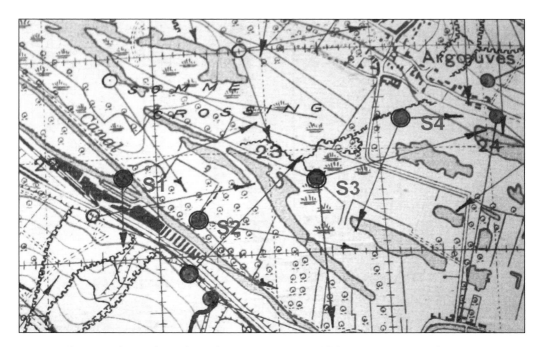

The map above shows how four GHQ pattern pill boxes, S1, 2, 3 and 4, were sited to guard the Somme river crossing west of Amiens, along with mobile machine guns. They were possibly constructed by 256th Tunnelling Company RE, with some assistance from 108th US Engineers attached for instruction, who recorded working in this area but gave little detail.

S1 (49.924110, 2.210344) can be found on the point of the island in the middle of the Somme, west of Amiens, covering any approach up the river or the banks. It is used today to house electrical equipment for the adjacent weir control.

S2 (49.921492, 2.214925) is on the bank of the Somme, also covering the river approaches. The river embankment has since been raised and partially obscures the apertures. This pill box shows signs of damage on one wall, either by 1918 or 1940 actions.

S3 (49.924255, 2.221094) has been partially submerged during extraction of aggregate and the subsequent erosion of the sub-ground, leaving it lying in the fishing lake.

S4 (49.926341, 2.225633) is in the public park in Argoeuves village. As it is constructed on soft ground, therefore liable to be less stable and able to withstand shellfire, the engineers have constructed it on a strong raised foundation in accordance with the specification.

S5 Coisy (49.956770, 2.327111).
One of the few surviving intact Moir Pill Boxes, in Coisy to the north of Amiens. It still has the protective steel revolving shield and the Vickers gun carriage suspended from the cupola. Sited on the GHQ Line, constructed probably by 144th Army Troops Company for the Australian Corps, it is located between the two marked lower centre on the map, marked S5, on the Rue des Peupliers.

There are remains of several other Moir Pill Boxes in the area. Because of the shape and dimensions, it has been common practice for local farmers to cement the inner bottom and then use the pill box as a cattle watering trough.

S6 (50.033558, 2.388647) west of Hérissart on the D60, is a good example. Sited on a trench line on an apex of high ground, it shows an excellent field of fire.

S7 (50.030076, 2.413674). The remains of the Moir Pill Box, now used as a cattle watering point, in Hérissart. Built probably by 221st Army Troops Company, it was sited to cover the eastern and southern approaches to the village.

S8, 50.060936, 2.415791 pictured below, next to the D11 north of Puchevillers, shows how the location gave a commanding field of fire over any approach from the east.

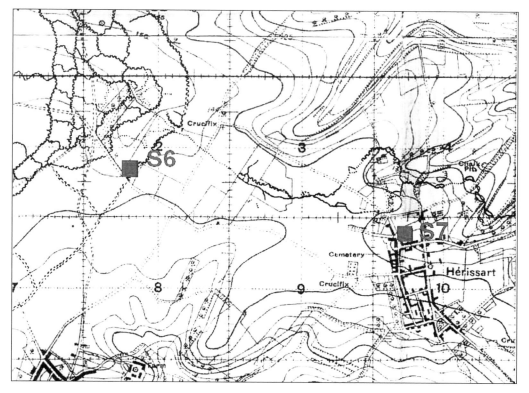

Map showing locations of S6, in the newly constructed trench line, and S7 at Hérissart.

S9A (50.100826, 2.478814)
S9B (50.100410, 2.479150),
S9C (50.100332, 2.479614)
are all Moir Pill Boxes
which have been converted
to cattle watering stations.
They are in a line, with about
50 yards between each,
crossing the D124 on the
high ground from
Vauchelles-les-Authie to
Authie, by the *chateau d'eau*
(water tower).

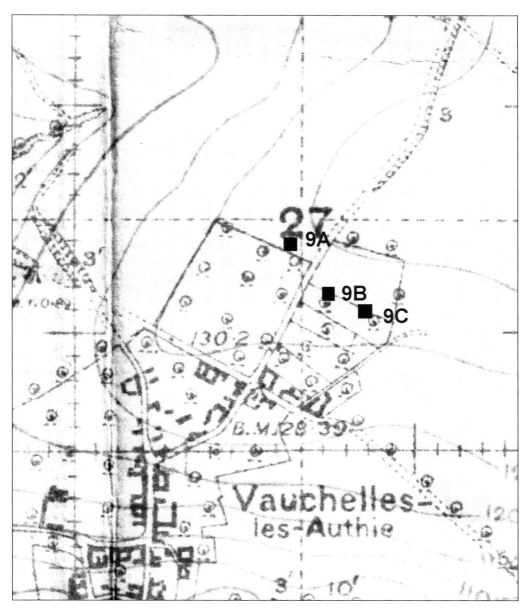

Map showing the three Moir Pill Boxes, S9A, S9B and S9C in the defence system on the high ground at Vauchelles-les-Authie.

S9D (50.089833, 2.471838) Vauchelles. In the trees beside the D124 going from Vauchelles to Arquèves, marked on modern IGN maps as Fosse d'Arquèves, is another Moir Pill Box structure which is part of the same defence system as those on the northern side of the village.

The Moir Pill Box was designed by Sir Edward Moir, an eminent engineer who was attached to the Ministry of Munitions. More detailed information is given in later pages.

In 1918 after the lines had settled following the German spring offensive, the Third Army sited and constructed strong defence lines, which included many concrete machine gun emplacements and artillery observation posts. Lacking the facility of a large pre-casting factory such as those operated by the First and Second Armies (they had established a small factory at Anzin, for the production of concrete burster blocks, drain pipes etc), they designed their own standard patterns of cast in-situ structures. Many of these still exist today and can be examined. They all have the same interior shapes and dimensions, being produced around standard formwork, with some varying external features dependent upon what materials were available. Intended for observation and described in one war diary as an 'artillery command post', they could also be used for machine guns. Constructed (some at trench level and some free-standing) by Army Troops Companies such as the 139th Company RE and 1st Siege Company Royal Anglesey Royal Engineers, for use by Corps artillery and machine gun units, many have since been demolished and cleared away. Those still existing are shown below.

S10 Arquèves (50.074366, 2.472353).
The pill box on the eastern side of Arquèves: the lines of sight and machine gun direction of fire is shown on the defences map below. The position on the crest gives a clear view over the land falling away to the south and east.

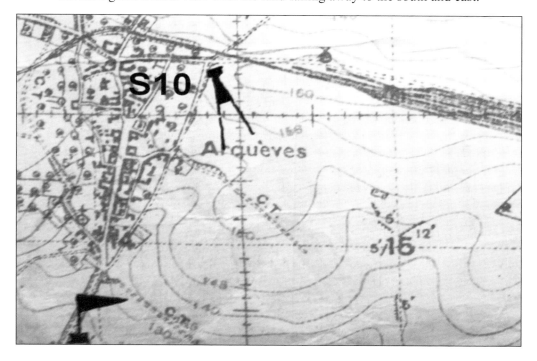

S11 Harponville (50.042355, 2.507640). An example of the same pattern is on the high ground north of the village, reached by passing the village church and the British cemetery. The location has an excellent field of view and, weather permitting, can maintain observation and dominate the land which the Germans might have been expected to try to infiltrate.

S12 Sailly-au-Bois (50.115314, 2.584593). To the south-west of Sailly-au-Bois, with good views over the area to the east held by the Germans at the extent of their 1918 offensive, is an identical structure. It was built, possibly by divisional troops of the 42nd Division, in the summer of 1918.

S13 Coigneux (Rossignol Farm) (50.133702, 2.559959). By the track from
Bayencourt to Rossignol farm, north of Coigneux, is another of the standard
Third Army pattern artillery observation posts, with good views over several
miles to the east. Shown as OP on the map.

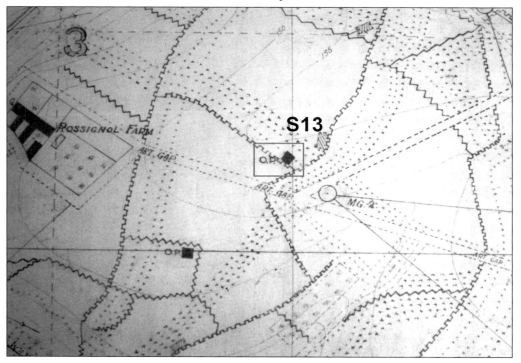

S14 Bayencourt (50.131745, 2.585950).
The map shows how this pill box was part of the Bayencourt Switch, with a field of fire to the east (black circle in centre)

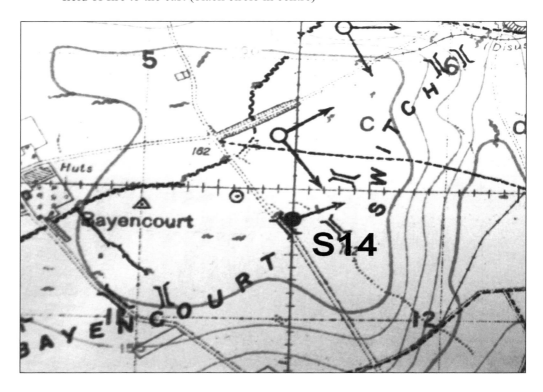

S15 Hébuterne (50.133292, 2.633409). Probably one of the most photographed pill boxes on the Somme which stands beside the D28 to the north of the village. It is sited on the trench which was the front line on 1 July 1916, the opening of the Battle of the Somme, and from where the 56th Division attacked Gommecourt Wood opposite. It has been reported elsewhere that this was used on the first day of the battle, however it was constructed in June or July 1918, part of the second line system at a strongpoint which had been O'Briens Post, possibly by the New Zealanders who held and strengthened the post in the summer of 1918 prior to being relieved by the 42nd Division. The map below, from summer 1918, shows O'Briens Post located on Richmond Trench.

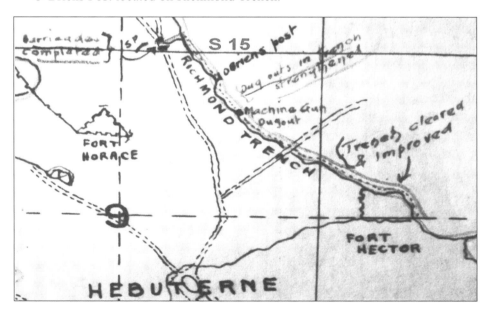

S16 (50.100023, 2.505183), S17 (50.099947, 2.504931) Louvencourt. By the side of the track running north-east out of Louvencourt is another example of the Third Army pattern, in the foreground, with a sunken concrete command post bunker, S17, in the background. It is sited on what was the Louvencourt Reserve system with commanding views over the area to the north-east and south-east.

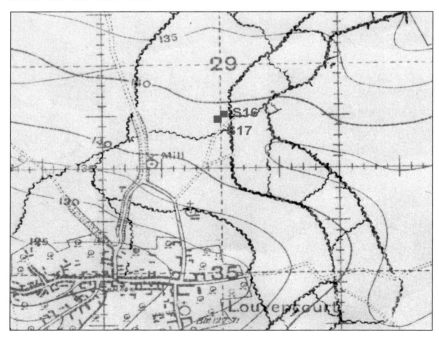

S18 Berles-au-Bois (50.190727, 2.629600). The existing concrete construction at Berles-au-Bois is shown on the trench map as artillery OP.

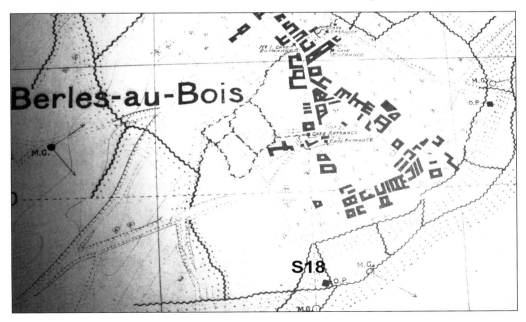

S19 Bienvillers-au-Bois South (50.168601, 2.625223). At the side of the road going southwards out of Bienvillers-au-Bois to Fonquevillers is an artillery observation post of the standard Third Army pattern. This survivor, one of the several around the village, is shown on the map below.

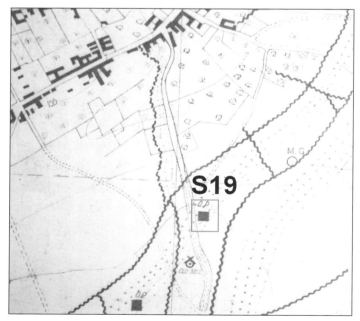

S20 Bienvillers-au-Bois North (50.180978, 2.623337).
In a small tree-lined field on the northern side of this village, by the D62 towards Berles-au-Bois, are the remains of a strongly built British machine gun pill box dating from 1918. The rear walls are of mass brickwork, in excess of a yard thick, with a reinforced concrete side and front walls with gun embrasure.

S21 Monchy-au-Bois (50.176850, 2.664785).
This was probably constructed by 565th (Wiltshire) Fortress Company Royal
Engineers and is the Moir recorded in the diary of the Chief Royal Engineer,
VI Corps, who visited this Chemin des Dames pill box during construction.
It was sited on the Monchy Switch trench, which utilised part of the OG (Old
German 1916) front line system. The steel rods which connected with and
anchored the steel cupola are evident and the structure shows signs of
damage, so it is likely that it was hit by a German shell and the roof blown
off.

S22, (50.223660, 2.716810), S23, (50.223807, 2.717206) Blairville. On the edge of the village, on the outer edge of the paddock by the entrance to the quarry works, can be found two concrete bunkers, constructed probably in July 1918 by 76th Field Company Royal Engineers of the Guards Division, on the site of a 1916 German trench.

S24 Mesnil-Martinsart (50.060693, 2.635061).
Just to the north of Mesnil Martinsart village, in a spur off a trench named Charles Avenue, are the concrete remains of another British observation post, also dating from 1918. This also gives excellent views over the German lines at Hamel and the Ancre valley. It appears to have been badly damaged by shell fire and is being further destroyed by tree roots. The location is identified by the tree, photo above.

S25 (50.060693, 2.635061), S26 (50.071956, 2.632685) Auchonvillers.
By the side of the D174 from Auchonvillers to Mesnil-Martinsart are two British bunkers which date from the summer of 1918. One is certainly built to house a machine gun, the other may be an observation post. They are sited on what was Bovet Trench in the second line, giving excellent views over the Germans then in the Newfoundland Memorial Park and Beaumont Hamel. The sandbag breastwork against which they were cast and stood can be easily identified.

S27 Pozières (50.026325, 2.719438).
On the track between Pozières and Contalmaison, built into the earth bank on the east side, is a brick and concrete shelter dating from 1916, probably constructed during the height of the Battle of the Somme. The roof of concrete is resting on piers of masonry bricks: such a construction would have been shrapnel proof but is unlikely to have withstood direct impact from a field gun shell.

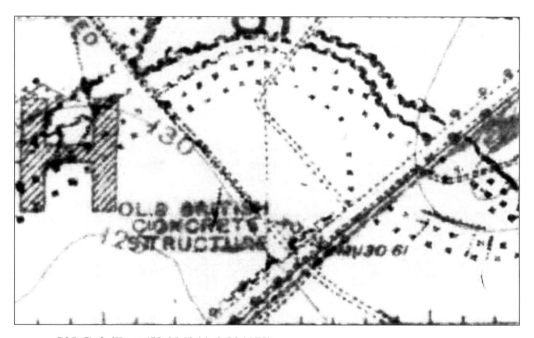

S28 Grévillers (50.096244, 2.824178).
The British bunker situated by the D929 Albert-Bapaume road near the Grévillers junction is likely to date from 1917 after the Germans had retired to the Hindenburg Line. Probably a command post for a heavy artillery section, it is sited behind the rising ground towards Bapaume, effectively out of sight of German observers.

S28 Grévillers (50.096244, 2.824178) continued
It has received a hit from an artillery shell, possibly in March 1918, although this has not caused major damage. The photographs below show front and rear views. It is marked on a trench map in mid 1918, when the area is again in Germans hands, and is identified as 'Old British Concrete Structure'.

S29 Colincamps (50.106336, 2.598658).
In July 1918 the 428th Field Company Royal Engineers of the 42nd Division began construction of a double machine-gun and observation post between Colincamps and Sailly-au-Bois (nowadays Ferme du Moulin, on the D23).
Their history records:

'On the 1st of July shift work was commenced on a concrete MG pill-box in a farm building near Colincamps in [map reference] J 30 b to which materials and water were carried every night by motor lorry. Corporal Boyes and his men showed great keenness, and surprised the many Staff Officers, who came to inspect operations very regularly, at the rapid rate of progress. About ten tons of material per day were put into this job, and it took about eighteen days to complete, with the addition of an Artillery Observation Post super-imposed upon it. As this building remained untouched by enemy shell fire, one cannot help wondering what the farmer decided to do on his return to his farm with a monolithic structure concealed in his barn with five-foot walls on top and sides, and whose foundations went three feet below ground level.'[9]

The two previous photographs show how the position looked shortly after the war and in recent times. The machine gun and OP apertures are still apparent.

The plan opposite, as drawn by the engineers carrying out the work, shows the layout and section of the main structure inside the barn, with a photo of the existing construction.

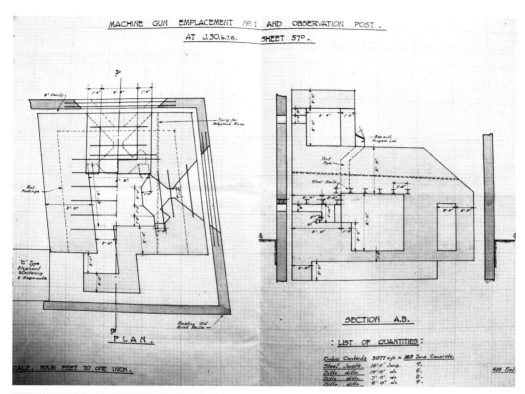

MACHINE GUN EMPLACEMENT № 1 AND OBSERVATION POST.
AT J.30.6.7.6.   SHEET 57ᴰ.

PLAN.

SCALE: FOUR FEET TO ONE INCH.

SECTION A.B.

: LIST OF QUANTITIES :

Cubic Contents 3077 c.ft. = 185 Tons Concrete.

Steel Joists	12'0" long.	5.
Ditto ditto	10'0" do.	6.
Ditto ditto	7'0" do.	2.
Ditto ditto	6'0" do.	4.

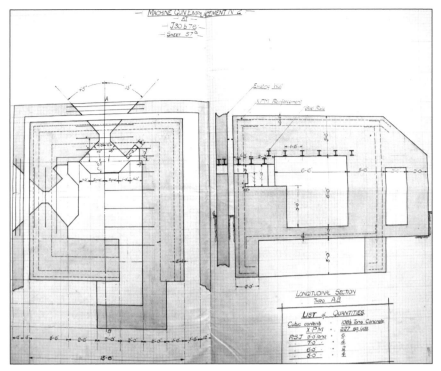

S29A (50.106588, 2.598594). Adjacent to the barn is the farmhouse, which was also converted into a machine gun post. Above is the engineer's drawing with recent photograph below. The two machine gun embrasures, in the end and side walls, can be seen; the end room of the house is uninhabitable, being solid concrete.

S30 Lassigny Farm (Ferme de Lassigny) (50.098271, 2.637030).
In the tree line on the edge of the field between the D918 and Lassigny Farm (known to the British as La Signy) is a concrete observation post which dates from the summer of 1918 when this formed the front line, named Jeremiah Trench, where it was joined by two communication trenches: Cheeron Trench, which had been used in 1916 and Newgate Street. The location in 1916 had been known as Ellis Square.

The ruins of the farmhouse and buildings at La Signy were occupied by the Germans and marked the furthest extent of their 1918 spring offensive. On 15 August it was reported that the Germans had retired from La Signy Farm, eastwards to beyond Serre, the information probably coming from this OP. It is likely that engineers of the 42nd Division, who held this sector and did much work in the area, constructed the post. It is a variation on the standard Moir pill box; being constructed right on the front line it would have been built at night and with difficult handling and placing of the materials. Until 2004 it was only possible to see the formed dome roof of the post. In 2004 an archaeological excavation partly uncovered the post and found it to be comprised partly of pre-cast blocks and partly in-situ concrete.

S31 Bresle (49.990925, 2.534430).

The bunker to the west of Bresle Wood was constructed as a signalling station for communication with forward posts. The flat roof enabled signals troops to set up and operate manual equipment, and also to take cover when needed. The strong shell-proof construction is marked as 'Rt. Group' on the map below, showing the posts to which it sent and received signals.

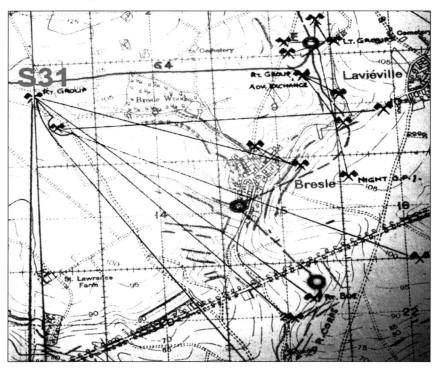

S32 Warloy-Baillon Mill (49.996995, 2.531705).
Near Baizieux, on the road towards Hénencourt, stand the ruins of Warloy-Baillon Mill. This was fortified by the British in 1918 with a concrete machine gun post, the shattered remains of which are still inside. The photos here show it today and at the end of the war.

S33 Mailly-Maillet Mill (50.098271, 2.637030).
To the north-east of the village, in a small copse by the side of the D919 towards Puisieux, is the remnant of Mailly-Maillet mill (marked on IGN maps as 'le Vieux Moulin Ruines'. The ruins consist largely of brick masonry and broken thick concrete walls, the remains of a British machine gun post. The mill was probably used as an observation post in 1916: the 247th Field Company Royal Engineers of the 63rd Division record erecting baffle walls in the mill for use as a machine gun post in July 1918. It was probably later hit and destroyed by German shell fire.

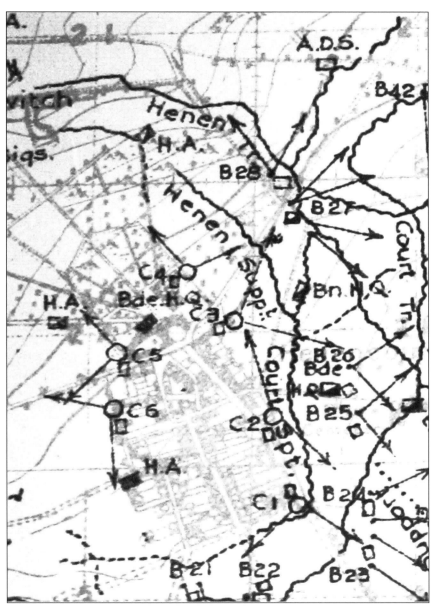

Map showing the 1918 defence scheme for Hénencourt. The machine gun pill boxes and observation posts, marked C1-C6, still exist today.

Hénencourt
S34-43 Hénencourt

This village, the headquarters of III Corps, was important to the British throughout 1916 with many troops resting here or passing through to the front. In 1918, after the German advance, the village was to be a point of strong resistance and was heavily fortified with a total of ten pill boxes constructed in the village and chateau grounds. All of these still exist, although not all are complete as whilst they were being built the front moved eastwards and they were left unfinished. Most work was carried out by Royal Engineer Field Companies attached to the 47th Division. The 520th Field Company recorded that, on 18th July 1918:

'we now took over work on the close defences of Hénencourt. This consisted of reinforced concrete MG and LG emplacements in accordance with Corps plans; we had the assistance of Infantry working parties for this, and not only were four sections fully employed, but we also had one section from each of the other two companies.'[10]

When they were relieved Lieutenant P.H. Wakefield RE, was left in charge of the work on the village defences. This field company re-started work on the pill boxes on 6 August, after three days work they were instructed to stop as work was required on the new front following the beginning of German withdrawal. Some of the pill boxes can be seen on the map which shows the early 1918 defence system around the village strongpoint, marked C1-C6.

The general pattern employed was along the lines of the standard GHQ design, but with variations. Although each pill box is of a slightly different shape, the general design, method of construction and reinforcement are all similar.

S34, (49.999881, 2.567813) by the side of the D119 road from Laviéville, shows the typical shape, with two machine gun embrasures. As with the others, the internal roof is strengthened with expanded steel mesh to reduce spalling from shell impact.

S35 (50.001481, 2.566981) is of similar design, although slightly smaller, and shows signs of being built into a brick building, now largely demolished.

S36 (50.002698, 2.565292) is in the basement of a private house which was an estaminet. The cellar was concreted with a machine gun field of fire which is now obscured by modern buildings.

S37 (50.004629, 2.565114) stands in the field with a good view towards Albert and the cathedral, then in German hands. In good light the Golden Virgin is clearly visible, especially in the afternoon when the sun is in the west. Its function was to provide signal communications for the brigade with battalions in the front lines, as shown on the map, marked 'RT. BGE. VISUAL ST'.

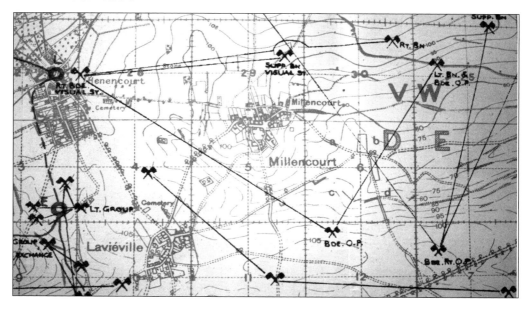

S38 (50.006381, 2.562786) is built into the perimeter wall of the chateau grounds. On the inside of the wall are the remains of the greenhouse, with the steel frame now derelict. The steel steps over the wall, probably built for gardeners' access, were built into the concrete construction. Below, the pill box also still has signs of military labelling and the rusting pivot bracket for a Vickers machine gun cast into the concrete.

S39 is in the chateau grounds, which is private property and access is not permitted.

S40 (50.004553, 2.560136) and S41 (50.004471, 2.560276) are only 25 yards apart; whereas S40 – which because of its shape and appearance has been wrongly described as being from World War Two – is clearly visible from the road in from Warloy-Baillon, S41 is partially hidden by the brick wall which is partly collapsed over the machine gun embrasure.

S42 (50.000592, 2.561684) stands on the edge of the village with good views and field of fire to the south-west.

S43 (49.998667, 2.562282) (not pictured) was partly complete, construction work being halted early in August 1918 when the British began forcing the Germans to the east at the start of the Hundred Days advance that led to the Armistice.

THE SOMME TO ARRAS

The locations of the Hénencourt pill boxes are marked on the map below.

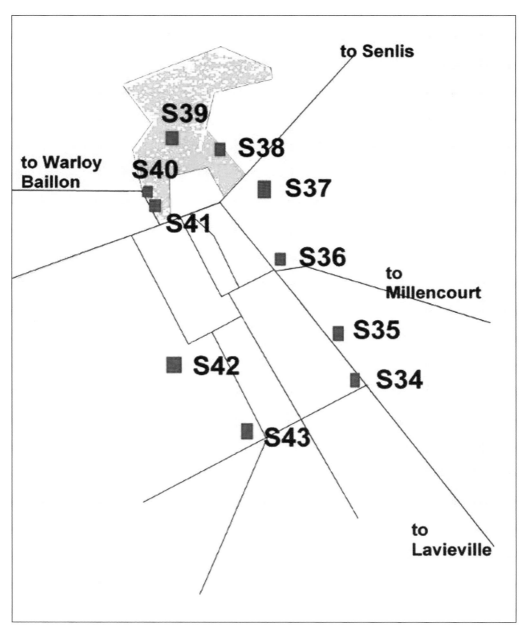

S44 (49.968006, 2.491155) S45, (49.966781, 2.491279) Franvillers.
The two bunkers west of Franvillers are the remains of a total of seven similar structures constructed by the 1st Australian Troops Company as part of the Lahoussoye system which was the reserve line. Started in late May 1918, this work continued through June before being handed over in July. All seven structures survived until the late 1990s, five being destroyed when the D929 was diverted around the village.

The pill box No.3 on the map and (below) as it was camouflaged.

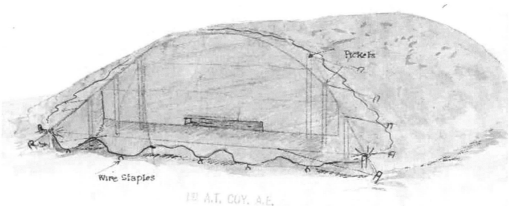

~ SKETCH OF FRONT CAMOUFLAGE ~
~ for M.G. Dugout. ~
(Assimilating mound of Earth.)

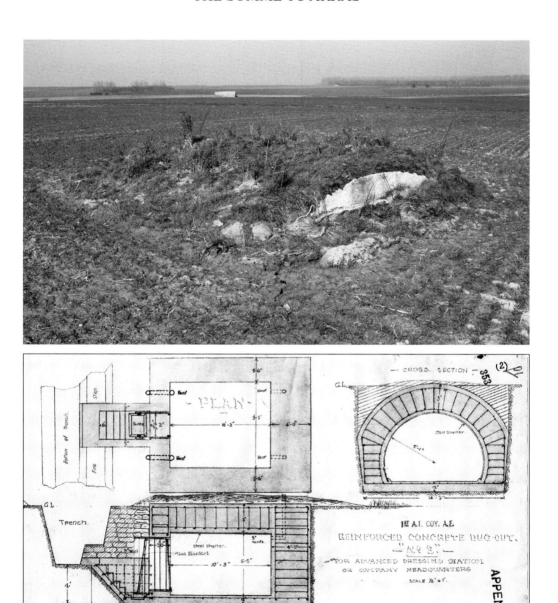

Plan and section of the bunker as designed as Advanced Dressing Station or Company HQ, It was later re-designated as a Lewis gun position.

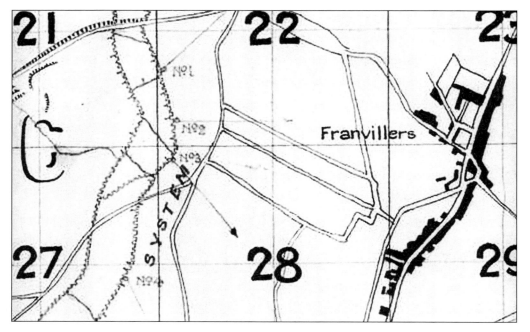

Section of trench map showing locations of No.1 (S44) and No.3 (S45) and their direction of fire.

S46 Key Wood (49.935588, 2.469285) Pont-Noyelles.
South of Lahoussoye the defence system line, which contained many dugouts and machine gun emplacements constructed by the Australians in 1918, continued down over the high ground in front of Pont-Noyelles and the valley in which sits Key Wood, marked on modern French maps as Bois de l'Ébouillère. In this wood (which is private property, used for hunting), is a concrete dugout of the same pattern as S45, marked on an engineer's map as infantry battalion HQ. Hidden under dense vegetation, it is impossible to photograph; it is marked on the French IGN Bleue series map.

CHAPTER 3

Cambrai

C1 Monchy-le-Preux (50.270601, 2.893334).
The Newfoundland Regiment Memorial, with the caribou atop, is built onto a British bunker, an observation post looking out over the German lines to the east of Monchy. Constructed after the village had been captured by the British 37th Division on 11 April 1917 by the New Zealand Tunnelling Company, these engineers recorded starting work on the observation post for heavy artillery in the doctor's house on 6 December, but concreting work was greatly delayed by frost and was not completed until 6 January 1918.

The observation post is quite unusual in that the steel facing is German, the New Zealand engineers appear to have re-cycled this probably from the western side of the village. This bull-nose steel plate pattern can be found in a number of German bunkers in the area.

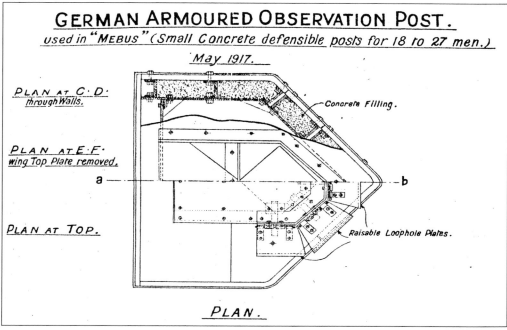

GERMAN ARMOURED OBSERVATION POST.
used in "MEBUS" (Small Concrete defensible posts for 18 to 27 men.)
May 1917.

PLAN at C·D·
through Walls.

Concrete Filling.

PLAN at E·F·
wing Top Plate removed.

a — — — — — — — — — — — — — — b

PLAN at TOP.

Raisable Loophole Plates.

PLAN.

C2 Vis-en-Artois (50.244282, 2.943263).

Not a concrete or shell-proof shelter, this existing shelter – an elephant-iron cupola with an earth covering – is typical of many constructed to give protection from aerial shrapnel bursts and the weather. Constructed into the lee of rising ground out of the Sensée valley, what was for a time the Canadian front line prior to their attack on the Drocourt-Quéant line, the German *Wotanstellung*, which ran on top of the slope, was for an infantry battalion and possibly used later as a Regimental Aid Post.

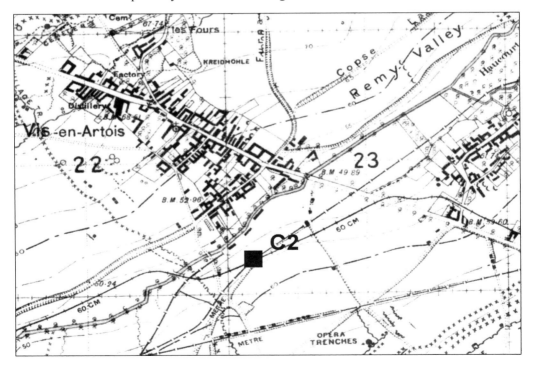

C3 Hermies (50.117458, 3.039554).
Similar to the preceding shrapnel-proof shelter, this partly-subterranean masonry and earth-covered elephant iron dug-out, with brick masonry front wall and inner walls, was about one mile behind the front line, which faced the Germans in the Hindenburg Line defences on the other side of the Canal du Nord. Built probably by engineers of the 36th (Ulster) Division who first occupied the village after the Germans fell back to their defences, this was the headquarters of 7th Lincolnshires who defended the British line here in March 1918.

It is believed that the shelter was later used as temporary post-war accommodation by returning civilians.

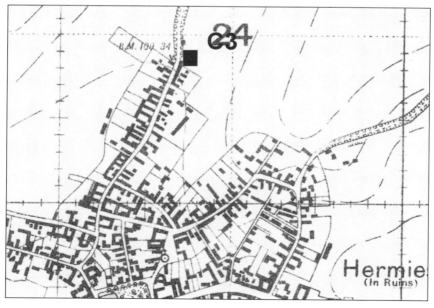

C4 Havrincourt Wood (50.089475, 3.075528).

Situated next to the main trackway through Havrincourt Wood, which was named Shropshire Spur by the British, is a brick-lined concrete dugout. Reached by concrete steps, it provided shell-proof cover – probably for a brigade HQ – which had been constructed by 150th Field Company Royal Engineers of 62nd Division as part of the planning for the forthcoming attack on the Hindenburg Line on 20 November 1917. Today it is largely full of debris and difficult to enter.

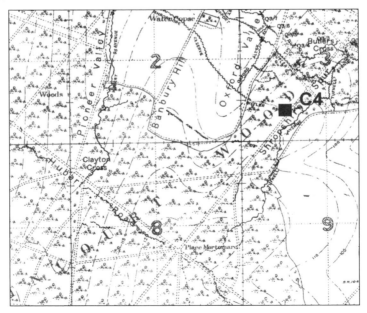

C5 Gouzeaucourt (50.053881, 3.124570).
One of the few pill boxes built by the British in this area to survive. Probably constructed by the 64th Field Company Royal Engineers of the 9th (Scottish) Division with some input by 234th Field Company of 39th Division, it was used by Scottish machine gunners who defended Gouzeaucourt on the morning of 21 March 1918.

The Germans had taken the village in their counter-attack of 30 November 1917 but held it only briefly before being pushed out by the Coldstream and Irish Guards. In February and March 1918, when the British were expecting a German offensive, the 9th Division bolstered the defence system and Gouzeaucourt was in the front line. The defences organised included machine guns in and around the village but they were unable to complete the work of making them shell-proof.

The Divisional Commander Royal Engineers, responsible for the work, recorded in his plans for defence of the village:

> 'Temporary emplacements have been made (and are occupied) for machine guns firing down High Street. Owing to sand not being procurable, the concrete work has not been started. Underground galleries are said to exist near the church, access being from a well, but this has not been found'.

The pill box was used throughout the day of 21 March 1918 when the Germans (120th and 123rd Württemberg Infantry Regiments) attacked after a heavy bombardment of gas and high explosive; the defences held until the evening when the defenders were ordered to retire.

C6 Gouzeaucourt Wood (50.058695, 3.088446).

The small masonry brick and concrete shelter in Gouzeaucourt Wood has recently been demolished: it seems the bricks had some value and have been taken, leaving little but a few bits of broken concrete and a small depression in the wood.

C7 (Morgan Post) Observation Post (50.011354, 3.126474) Épehy.

Built within the original farmhouse, with good views over the German lines for artillery spotting and direction, this tower shows signs of being hit by German artillery but the core has remained intact.

The pattern of the outer steel formwork is apparent. It was constructed by Royal Engineers who reportedly had American engineering troops attached to them for instruction in the winter of 1917/18. The village was held by the 21st Division, including the Leicestershires, when the Germans attacked and they held the enemy back. Around the OP there would have been much hand-to-hand and small arms fighting before the defenders were pushed back.

The pictures above and left show the front and rear views.

C8 Cullen Post (50.005348, 3.134741) Épehy.
This tall observation tower on the eastern edge of Épehy, on Rue Louis Georges, was described as a 'visual station' when constructed by 126th Field Company RE prior to the German attack in March 1918, and also consists of Rye's plates with a concrete core. This was Cullen Post, Épehy, built to provide good views over the German lines down Lark Valley, marked on modern French maps as Vallée des Trois Arbres. Front and rear views are shown here.

It was constructed using Rye's Plates, a system of permanent shell-proof formwork for the easy erection of tall structures, mainly as observation posts for artillery and intelligence. The plate was devised to meet the demands of the artillery for easily erected observation posts which were resistant to shell fire. The plate was made in two lengths, 6 feet and 9 feet, and shaped and holed for easy bolting. After the plates were connected as required the inner core was filled with concrete, which need not contain steel reinforcement. The standard Rye's Plate and system of bolting together, with rails for anchoring to foundation and forming floor and roof support, is shown below.

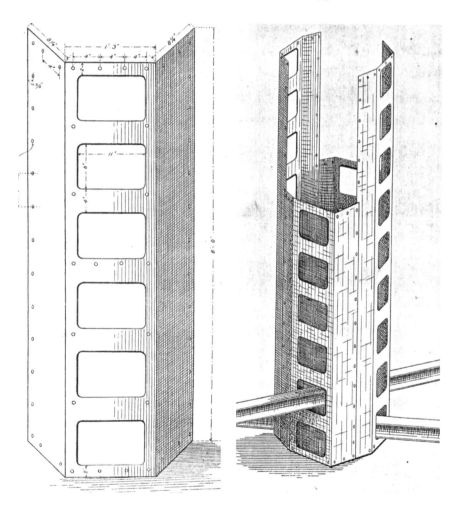

Some of the many designs which were possible, depending upon the pattern of bolting employed, can be seen below.

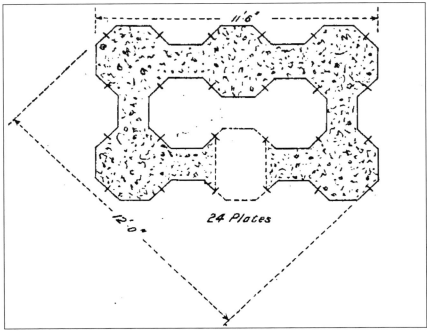

24 Plates

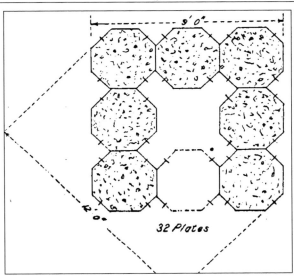

32 Plates

Engineers of the 4th New Zealand Field Company constructed at Surrey Farm (Zurrey Farm) near Frelinghien, in August 1917, an artillery observation post comprising Rye's plates with a concrete core.

The engineers reported that the post *'was daily shelled with medium and heavy artillery shells for over two months without being destroyed and was used continuously'*. It does not remain today. Although the New Zealanders were happy with the Rye's Plates, the Australians were not. The Commander Australian Engineers inspected some OPs which had been built, did not like them and said in his diary, *'I consider RYE plates should never be used for this work if it can be avoided'*. He then had some sketches drawn which showed the plates used but with an outer casing of reinforced concrete.

Two views – on p.75 and above – of Hasler House observation post, St Jean, near Ypres. Constructed in 1916/17 for Royal Artillery by 6th Siege Company, Royal Monmouthshire Royal Engineers, it is in a house which was later shelled several times. The Rye's plates can be seen, photographed in 1918 and a year or two later.

Due to the structural strength and solidity of the towers built with the plates, several survived repeated hits from artillery shells and remained as high vestiges after the war, with their height making them unmistakable in villages which were being cleared and rebuilt. The example below shows one in Gonnelieu, when the village was being resettled.

C9 Ronssoy (private location).
Built into what had been a barn on the eastern side of the main street, Chaussée Brunehaut, D58, this example was not damaged during the war, and the barn was re-built around the structure.

The photos show the barn, where the lower part of the post can be seen through the doorway, and the internal post, now whitewashed, which extends up into the attic. It stands in private property.

77

C10 Ronssoy (private location).
In the same village, also on private property off the main road, is another post using the Rye's Plate system, showing how it formed permanent formwork when filled with concrete. This example, rear view above, which had been built into a building destroyed by German artillery, shows some severe damage to the steel work but the structure withstood the shell hits.

C11 Lempire(49.990180, 3.164760).

Situated in the angle of a small by-road which is off the D28 Lempire-Vendhuile road, partly hidden by undergrowth and slippage of the bank it was built into, is a concrete reinforced elephant iron shelter. With a covering of brickwork and earth, this was the battle headquarters of 2nd Royal Dublin Fusiliers when the Germans opened their spring offensive on the adjoining villages of Lempire and Ronnsoy. The area around the dugout was held until the defenders were outflanked by the Germans.

C12 Wancourt (50.245428, 2.873976).
This British shelter was constructed during the Battle of Arras, once the Germans had been pushed out of the village and over the high ground of Wancourt Hill behind. It is not a strong construction and the roof, which consisted of steel girders, has been demolished. The solidity can be compared to the German bunker 50 metres away. This has very thick shell-proof walls and roof, being constructed when the front lines were several miles away to the west, materials were easily transported and there was little danger or disruption, unlike the Royal Engineers, who were working under constant bombardment.

C13 Gauche Wood (50.040852, 3.135524).
Gauche Wood, just west of Villers-Guislain, had been in the area abandoned by the Germans in their falling back to the Hindenburg Line, and was left further back when the British attacked and took land from the Germans during the opening of the Cambrai offensive. However the wood was back in German hands a few days later when they launched their counter-attack although before long they in turn were forced out by the 1st Guards Brigade.

The wood, which by this time had few trees and thin undergrowth, now formed a sharp salient in the front line. It was to form an important point of defence and several machine guns were sited there. To provide shelter for the machine gun crews of the 90th Field Company RE constructed in January 1918 the shelter which is there today. This housed the crew of 27th Machine Gun Company who held off the German attack which started the spring offensive on 21 March 1918.

Nearby can be found an identifiable section of Lancashire Trench, from when the Lancashire battalions (South and Loyal North) of the 55th Division defended the wood in November 1917. In March 1918 it formed the British front line of the 9th Division.

CHAPTER 4

North of Arras

The area north and west of Arras, with the exception of the splendid and moving Vimy Ridge Memorial Park (which does not appear in this listing as the concreted trenches are a reconstruction), does not attract many battlefield visitors, although there is much to see, especially the 1918 defences.

In anticipation of the German offensive which came in the spring of 1918 the British bolstered the defences north and west of Arras, which formed parts of the Corps and GHQ Lines. Along the line which ran from Frévin-Capelle, past Maisnil and Gouy-Servins to Bouvigny-Boyeffles are six remaining large, solid and well constructed machine gun pill boxes, all built to the same design with minor modifications. They are similar to the standard GHQ pattern but with some differences, such as lack of rear entrance protection and no facility to fire from behind, over the roof. Also lacking is the amount of ventilation provided in the GHQ pattern.

N1 Frévin Capelle (50.040770, 3.136725).
The concrete machine gun emplacement on the rising ground south of the railway line at Frévin Capelle is a very solid and shell-proof structure for two machine guns. Today a farm road, running parallel with the rail line, passes close by. Still with the earth covering placed for camouflage, it has commanding views over the approaches from the east. The siting was on a trench line planned to run in front of the main GHQ defence line.

Further north a number of pill boxes which formed the GHQ Line in front of Gouy-Servins are still to be found. These are shown below on the contemporary British map, which has no trenches or lines marked.

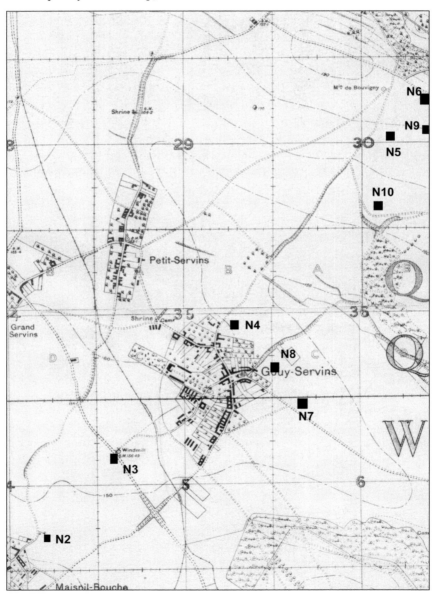

N2 Maisnil (Maisnil Bouche) (50.395805, 2.637534).

The exterior shape, with squared lower walls and rounded upper, as can be seen on those at Maisnil, is due to the type of formwork available rather than any design effect. This one also still shows signs of camouflage work: rendered/painted front face and steel hooks cast into the roof to which camouflage netting was attached. The map below shows the existing machine gun emplacement (shown as No.56 on the sector map below) and how it formed a part of the defence of Maisnil-Bouche village and the GHQ Line.

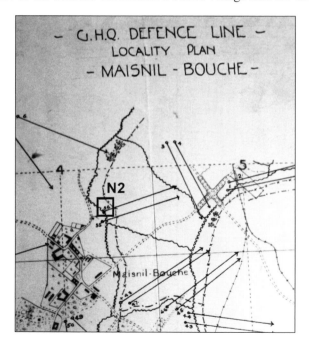

N3 Maisnil (50.399224, 2.642384).
Adjacent to the D65 Villers-au-Bois to Servins road is another, of similar design and probably by the same construction unit.

N4 Gouy-Servins (50.405912, 2.652340).
The one at Gouy-Servins differs from the others in a way which has not been seen on many other Great War British pill boxes – the provision of an overhead cover to the machine gun embrasure which can be seen to the left in the photograph below. Two other examples of this type stand in fields close by.

N5, (50.413673, 2.663294), N6 (50.415792, 2.665955) Bouvigny-Boyeffles.
This defence line also contained another type of machine gun post of which
some still remain.

N7 (50.401785, 2.656921), N8 (50.404346, 2.653858) Gouy-Servins.
On the east side of the village is a pair of square machine gun pits of unusual pattern. Sited at parapet level and double-skinned, they have a 9 inch air gap to reduce the effects of concussion on the inner skin and occupants in the event of an artillery hit to the front or sides. The ground level loophole, with a steel beam lintel, is well below the upper edge and through both skins. The design, seen as a speedy method of producing emplacements, was sanctioned at a conference of Chief Engineers at Second Army headquarters in May 1918:

'It was agreed that there was no time to put in Pill Boxes. Concrete lined open boxes sunk in the ground with weatherproof cover were suggested for MG emplacements.'

These remaining emplacements were almost certainly constructed for Canadian machine gun crews by Canadian engineers, probably men of 4th

Canadian Army Troops Company who recorded excavating and constructing open MG emplacements in the area. The diary of the Reconnaissance Officer, Machine Gun Office Canadian Corps, for May 1918 records that similar *'square pits with machine gun tables should be camouflaged'*.

The positions have a commanding view over the land to the east. The reconnaissance officer also gives advice that *'Positions will normally be sited clear of definite trench lines. Every endeavour should therefore be made to take advantage of natural covered approaches...forward guns should be sited in pairs.'*[11]

N9 (50.411232, 2.661910), N10 (50.413598, 2.665606).
Another pair of the same design and construction is to be found about 1,000 metres to the northeast, also with advantageous views towards the front line.

N11 Habarcq (50.300648, 2.610039).

On the edge of the village of Habarcq, which being on a slight rise was an important place to defend, can be found the lower section of a Moir Pill Box, the sole remaining vestige of the many pill boxes which were in this area. As with many others in the south, the top has been removed to provide a watering point for cattle, this alteration being the likely reason it was not demolished with the others.

Habarcq was an important village on the GHQ Line and was well defended with many machine gun posts. This remaining one, with a good field of fire over the valley, is sited on what was a local tramway, which came up the slight cutting which can be seen in the middle and background. The trench map below shows how it was on the front line trench of the GHQ Line defence system.

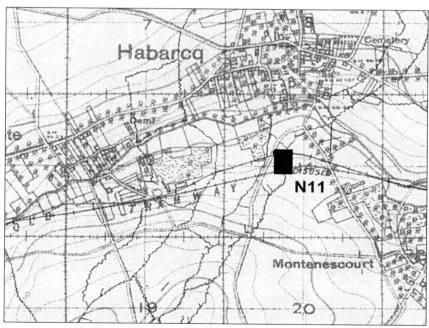

N12 Souchez (50.384813, 2.753674).

As pre-cast concrete was known to offer some advantages over in-situ concrete, both in terms of speed of construction and quality of work, and eliminated the need for shuttering, mixing or steel joists and rails, a trial was carried out in Zouave Valley, (marked on modern maps as Vallée des Zouaves) south of Souchez, on land recently captured from the Germans. In October and November 1917, 230th Army Troops Company of the Royal Engineers constructed concrete walls of various beam and reinforcement designs. The trials – to assess the effect of a direct hit by an 18lb shell fired from close range – were carried out on 18 December in the presence of senior officers. These results influenced British designs and confirmed the benefits of pre-casting.

It was estimated that whereas an in-situ concrete pill box might take up to two weeks to construct, and would require at least another two weeks before the concrete gained sufficient strength to resist shell fire, a pre-cast one would take about four to five days and would be useable almost immediately.

Some of the test pieces from the trials at Souchez which remain today.

CHAPTER 5

Arras to Armentières

A1 La Rutoire (50.481359, 2.765753) Vermelles.
The observation post in the farmyard at La Rutoire, showing obvious signs of being cast against corrugated iron sheeting, gave views towards the front lines at Loos. The apertures are too high for machine gun operation. As the front was fairly static for some time here the OP could date from several periods, although it probably is from some time in 1916.

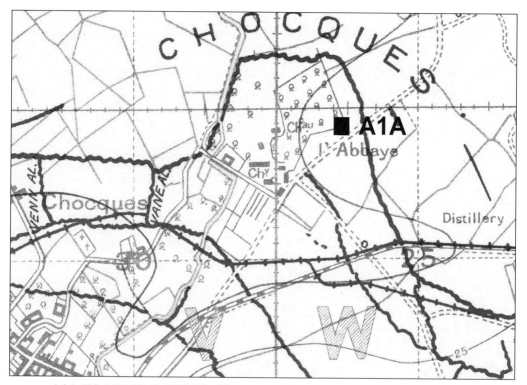

A1A (50.547799, 2.587066). Chocques Abbey.
Built into the boundary wall of the abbey is a pill box which was on the Reveillon-Chocques Line. It was built behind the brickwork of the wall for camouflage, which has since fallen away, leaving the masonry imprint with machine gun apertures exposed. The 42nd Army Troops Company RE recorded building this as part of XIII Corps' defences. A large and substantial structure, with two chambers for three machine guns, ventilation could be provided by means of the metal pipe which can be seen exiting the far doorway. On the following page are front and rear views. The abbey in whose grounds it was built is now derelict and the land is used by a horse stabling and riding school.

A2 Le Quesnoy (Beuvry) (50.534575, 2.682453).

The village of Le Quesnoy had been a keep or strongpoint in 1916 and in 1918 it was maintained as such with the expectation and eventuality of a German advance: it was held up by the 55th Division at Givenchy. A shelter for the brigade which had its HQ next to the strongpoint was built into a building which was here, probably a small house. The road is nowadays named Rue Lucien-Trinel. On the edge of the small spinney is the double chambered bunker, very poorly constructed and with little apparent strength. It shows signs of having been constructed of poorly constituted concrete and

needing internal repairs to prevent ceiling collapse and rain penetration. It is unlikely to have withstood a hit from even a small shell. It is pictured above, and the location is given on the map, next to Le Quesnoy strongpoint, as one of two brigades under Corps control.

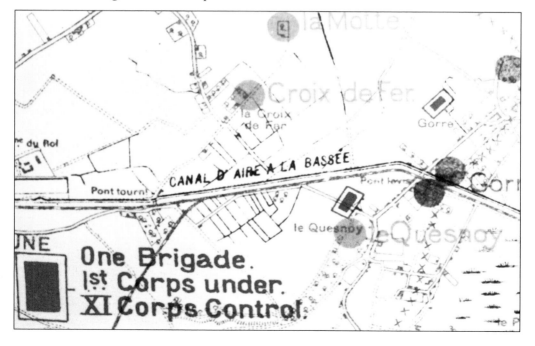

A2A Hinges (Le Cauroy) (50.572523, 2.608497).
This single-chamber bunker is at the location of what was one of Twin Farms, (the other was on the opposite side of the road, still discernible as an overgrown patch) between Le Cauroy (on modern maps Le Corroy) and Les Harisoires. The original masonry is evident. A single chamber without loophole, with a 4 feet thick roof supported by steel rails, it is sited on the Suffolk Line, part of the Hinges-Bethune Line, which was part of the defence system for Mont Bernanchon, a rise which gave good views and needed to be denied to the Germans. The 42nd Army Troops Company commenced work on what they termed a 'concrete dugout' on 17 June 1918. After completion it was used by a signals unit of XIII Corps who were holding the line here. An almost identical shelter stood further up the high ground, by the D937, until demolished in about 2005.

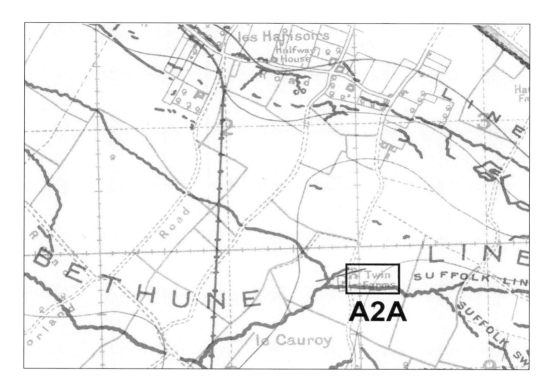

A3 Festubert (50.540449, 2.737151).

The large, solid bunker with open chambers was known as Tramways House, an important point on the light rail system, Barnton Tramway, which ran between the front line and the Tuning Fork area (named after the road junction of that shape) towards Gorre. The adjacent road junction was named Ration Corner, with rail sidings immediately opposite on the other side of the D166. It was built into what was the last building (the original house brickwork is still evident) before the open, flat and featureless country behind and up to the front lines.

The 427th RE Field Company of 42nd Division in December 1917 record constructing this. They:

'concentrated on the provision of ferro-concrete shelters in the third-line defence known as the Village Line. These shelters were made by placing heavy corrugated iron sheets bent to the shape of part of a circle and bolted together, in the rooms of the houses, and building

over them walls 3 feet thick and roof 4 feet thick of ferro-concrete. However the few that were completed were found to be 5.9-inch shell-proof and helped the 55th Division three months later to make their famous stand against the big German offensive.'[9]

The map below shows how Tramways House at Ration Corner was used as a Bearer Relay Post by the medical services, between the Regimental Aid Post at Barnton Road and the ADS at Tuning Fork.

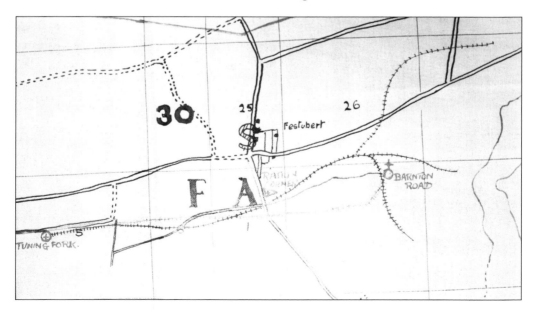

A4 Le Plantin (50.534459, 2.741664), Festubert.

A standard English shelter in Festubert village, this was the Battalion HQ of the 1/7th Kings Liverpool Regiment before and during the fighting around Festubert. From here much of the fighting in the vicinity was commanded by battalion staff in April 1918, who organised a counter-attack when the Germans broke through and re-captured Windy Corner, the road junction just south.

The bunker was constructed probably by 428th/429th Field Company in December 1917; it was reported that materials froze in the sub-zero temperature and work was delayed until the thaw. The incorporation of sandbags as formwork and adjoining sandbag shelters is evident from the side wall construction and also the imprints on the interior, which is today used for coal storage.

This company did much work in this sector and recorded their efforts in carrying materials for just a few of their constructions – 34,112 sandbags, each weighing 60lbs – which had been brought up from the RE dump at Gorre.

Job No.	Name of Shelter.	Internal Dimensions of Dug-out.			Material (Sandbags Full).			
		Lgth.	Wth.	Max Hght.	Shingle.	Sand.	Cement.	Total.
1.	Spoil Bank Keep	8′ 9″ × 4′ 9″ × 5′ 3″			2645	1323	712	4680
2.	Oxford Terrace No. 1 Coy. H.Q.	8′ 9″ × 4′ 9″ × 5′ 3″			2784	1392	744	4920
3.	Oxford Terrace No. 2 Co. H.Q.	8′ 9″ × 4′ 9″ × 5′ 3″			2784	1392	744	4920
4.	Orchard Keep Co. H.Q.	16′ 0″ × 7′ 0″ × 5′ 3″			3925	1963	1048	6936
5.	Kingsclere Bt. H.Q. Buzzer Stn.	7′ 9″ × 4′ 9″ × 5′ 3″			1525	763	360	2648
6.	Pill Box II. Tower Res. Trench	10′ 4″ × 4′ 9″ × 5′ 3″			1907	953	476	3336
7.	Pill Box III. Nr. La Bassée Road	10′ 4″ × 4′ 9″ × 5′ 3″			1907	953	476	3336
8.	Pill Box IV. Marylebone Road	10′ 4″ × 4′ 9″ × 5′ 3″			1907	953	476	3336

CONCRETE WORK IN RIGHT SECTOR OF LA BASSÉE FRONT, SHOWING MAN LOADS FOR EACH JOB IN HAND.

Average weight of Sandbags, 60 lbs.

Thickness of concrete on top or enemy side, 5 feet.

GIVING A TOTAL IN MAN LOADS OF 34,112.

Fleurbaix
A5 Fleurbaix (50.660357, 2.823626).
This is a large concrete shelter on the northern side of Fleurbaix near Port à Clous farm. It is not of the same design or construction as the others in Fleurbaix, having a rear entrance with covered doorway: it does not have an embrasure or fitting for machine gun. It was probably built in July 1917 by 502th (Wessex) Field Company for 170 Infantry Brigade HQ as Fleurbaix was constantly shelled. Later it was used as a command post by 12th Suffolk and remnants of 121 Brigade of 40th Division during the German attack on 9 April 1918. For twenty-four hours this post formed part of the front line, being almost surrounded, until the remnants of the force defending it fell back to Bac St Maur.

The map below shows the village as a defended locality, intended to break up any attacking force. The crossed squares marked are concrete machine gun posts, all built to a pattern. There were nine in and around the village. As late as 5 April 1918, only days before the expected attack, the 229th Field Company chose a site to erect another, but this work was not carried out. Three of the posts still exist; the others which survived the war have been demolished for housing schemes, one in recent years.

   Two of these remaining were used by Lewis gunners of the 12th Suffolks who held off the Germans for most of the day before being forced to retire as they were cut off as troops on either side of them were pushed back by the German onslaught.

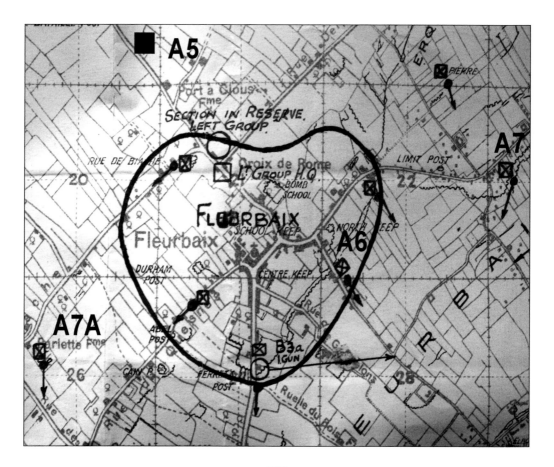

A6 (50.651011, 2.839344), the emplacement southeast of the village, by the D176.

Of similar design, but with extra protection to the rear entrance, this was constructed by Lieutenant C.L. Hale with No.3 section of 421st Field Company RE, who recorded this work on 21 March as constructing a *'concrete machine gun shelter'*. The engineers did not have an easy time of it. They record great difficulties in getting materials forward to site because of shelling and road damage furthermore, during construction the area was shelled and saturated with gas. This pill box played a large part in the fighting around Fleurbaix when the German attack began.

The large slabs of concrete on the roof are from other emplacements which were destroyed during the fighting and later.

A7 (50.655304, 2.851757). The easternmost of the surviving structures, constructed of an elephant-iron inner lining with a thick reinforced concrete roof and protected side entrances.

A7A Fleurbaix (50.646784, 2.816373).
The emplacement at Barlette Farm on the D174 west of the village was used by machine gunners of 119 Brigade until evacuated with the German advance. A direct artillery hit which did little damage illustrates the strength of the construction. The adjacent farmhouse which formed part of the same strongpoint, Barlette Farm, had been an Advanced Dressing Station until it was made shell-proof for Brigade HQ prior to the expected attack. The emplacement was manned by the machine gunners and 12th Suffolks of 40th Division who held the Germans back until forced to retire:

'At 12 noon hostile forces had penetrated just south of Croix Blanche and were moving in considerable numbers on Barlette Farm. Here Lt Bain and 2nd Lt Ellis with the gun brought back by Cpl Wallace and with 50 infantry whom they had collected, put up a most determined stand but finally fresh parties of the enemy came into action against them with Light Machine Guns from the rear, and orders being received from the G.O.C. 119th Infantry Brigade they fell back.'

'Fleurbaix meanwhile, though practically surrounded, was holding out.'[12]

A8 (50.572523, 2.608497), A9 (50.555765, 2.675444) Le Hamel.
At the far end of the field behind the farm on Rue de la Goutte, east of Essars, one in each corner, are two machine gun posts which comprised a post or strongpoint named Le Hamel NW. They are both of the same design, constructed using house bricks with a thick concrete roof to a standard pattern by 145th Army Troops Company RE in the autumn of 1917. Rather more resistant to shell-fire than might be expected from a house brick building, it is a double-skin design; an outer skin is provided to take the full force of a shell with an air space and then another layer several courses thick. There is also solid brickwork to the front of the aperture giving extra protection against a hit. They were made to accommodate a machine gun crew of two men.

   Part of I Corps defences, they are sited to protect any forward approach between the Lawe and Aire Canals and were used by troops of XI Corps during the German push forward on 11th April 1918.

The map below shows them (Le Hamel NW) as a single strongpoint or post as part of the Le Hamel Switch, in the Beuvry-Gorre Line. Also shown on the map is the strongpoint named Gorre Wood, which comprised two machine gun posts, the following two entries, A10 and A11.

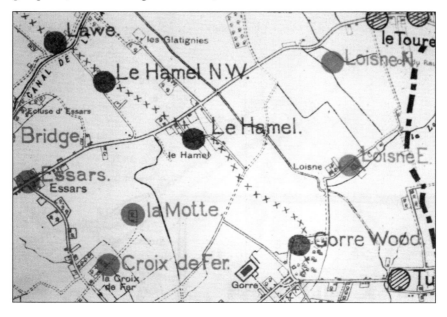

A10 Gorre Wood (50.543027, 2.696167).
In the north-west corner of Gorre Wood, the grounds of Gorre chateau, which was Divisional HQ, is another two-man masonry brick circular pill box of the same design as the two at Essars. It is shown above, with an inside view below with gun aperture. The lower ledge is to accommodate the Vickers machine gun trestle and feet with embrasure above.

A10A Gorre Wood (50.543320, 2.699171).
A rear view of the other pill box in Gorre Wood. Unlike the other one close by, this is of cast in-situ concrete with a cubic shape, but with similar gun aperture. Whereas both are sited just inside the wood, they are behind the tree line by about 20 yards, making it more difficult for German artillery to locate them on maps. They were used for the defence of Loisne during the attack of 9/10 April 1918.

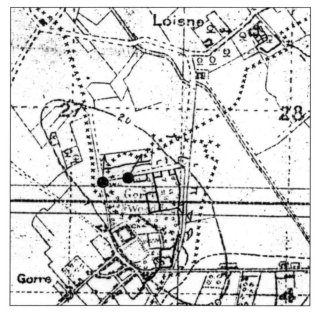

The maps below show the positions of the two individual pill boxes, inside the northern edge of the wood, with their main field of fire and how they are sited to cover gaps in the wire, which were located to channel attackers.

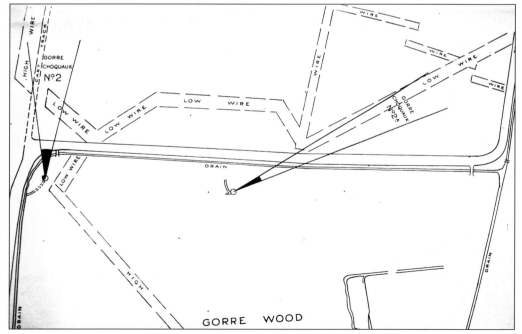

A11 La Couture (50.582058, 2.716954).

This is the one remaining pill box of the several constructed for the defence of La Couture, a village which was a defended locality and expected to hold off any strong attack. It was held by the Portuguese Division, most of whom left the village when the Germans attacked on the morning of 9 April 1918. The Cyclists Battalion arrived and later the Seaforths, and held the post and the area around the pill box, assisted by some of the Portuguese who had not fled but stayed and fought, with the attackers getting very close but being held back by machine guns in and around the pill box. It is today sealed for the conservation and protection of the bats which have made a home inside.

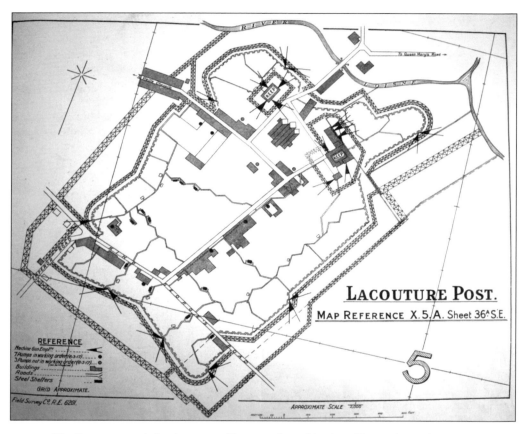

The Portuguese defenders are still remembered in the village; the main street, the D169, is named Rue du Colonel Bento Roma, after their officer who rallied the troops, and the Portuguese memorial stands near the church.

A11A Le Touret (50.56014, 2.72952).

By the side of the D171, Rue du Bois, just east of Le Touret, hidden in the long grass on the northern side of the road opposite the roadstone chipping dump, can be seen the domed roof of a concrete construction which was probably the shelter for a railway operating unit. At this point two tramway lines – Rue du Bois Tramway, which went south eastwards to the front lines, and one which ran north eastwards to the front, met and a crew would have been required to maintain the points and junction. The tramways terminated just to the west, directly opposite Le Touret British Cemetery, and it is quite likely that many of the dead and wounded would have been unloaded here.

The bunker was captured by the Germans during the Battle of the Lys in April 1918, after a determined defence by the 55th Division, and for that summer it was just behind their lines and would have been used as cover from British fire.

A12 Gorre (50.542817, 2.712282).
The 1/6th Battalion Liverpool Regiment was here during the fierce fighting for the defence of Givenchy in April 1918. It had been used by several battalions, and signallers, beforehand. When the attack began the Liverpools recorded: *'Battalion HQ was established in the Corps Signal dugout behind the farm house at* [map reference] *X28d 9.3'*. The area around the bunker was subject to heavy shelling with gas and high explosive for several days.

The bunker was concreted by 468 Field Company Royal Engineers. It is of typical English shelter construction (the iron lining is well preserved, as is the timber formwork to the interior of the rear wall), with the addition of a small entrance lobby and a window and stove pipe vent at the other elevation.

A13 Gorre (50.538907, 2.713264).
Nearby is a small bunker, probably an ammunition store for the several machine gun positions which were here at the road junction known as the Tuning Fork.

A14 King's Post (50.535267, 2.724459) Festubert.
In the yard of a private house down the track named Rue des Malvaux, in the woods west of Festubert, is a large and solid bunker, named King's Post, built by 419th Field Company Royal Engineers of the 55th (West Lancashire) Division after they had stopped the German advance and the line had stabilised. Built as a brigade HQ, it was probably named after the King's (Liverpool) Regiment, which had six battalions in the division.

A15-21 Festubert (Woods) (50.536426, 2.730532).
In the marshy wooded area just west of Festubert, behind houses on the Rue du Plantin, is a group of seven shelters, all constructed to house units of the 55th Division in the summer of 1918. Each bunker, most covered in ivy, has the imprint of the divisional emblem, the red rose of Lancashire, cast into the concrete by the doorway. Some of the imprints still show traces of the red paint. The photographs following show some of the bunkers and the divisional emblems.

117

118

A22 Nieppe (Nippon Bend) (50.698656, 2.807624).
Along the un-numbered road (Rue de Menegatte) that runs from Nieppe to Steenwerck in the area between the railway line and the A25 Autoroute, is a British bunker, probably an artillery command post built by engineers of the 46th Division, which was used during the Battle of Estaires until it was captured by the Germans on 12 April 1918. The farm in 1917 had been an ammunition storage area established by the Australians. The structure is larger than a normal bunker of its type, with a low level entrance lobby reached by steps, which shows signs of being covered by a wooden canopy the shape of which can be discerned in the concrete. Although partially flooded, the interior still contains much of the original wood lining and framing.

CHAPTER 6

Hazebrouck

H1 Mont Bernanchon (50.590757, 2.586690).

The village atop this high ground, looking over the land towards Lestrem and La Bassée, also gave good views over the land to the west and had to be denied to the Germans. It was well defended, with the advantage of the Aire Canal in front of it. The last remnant of the Hinges-Mont Bernanchon defences, this large and solid pill box was built into what was Brass Hat Farm probably by 431st or 432nd Field Company of 66th Division.

H2 Les Amusoires, (50.605818, 2.565431) which consists of a couple of small farms and a few houses which straddle the un-numbered road parallel to the D937 between Robecq and St Venant, formed the southern section of the Amusoires-Haverskerque Line. Here there were a number of First Army Aire pattern concrete block and beam pill boxes, some of which are still there. This example was, and still is, built into the end of the farmer's barn, with a good field of fire over the flat land.

A few yards away, across the farmyard, the garage has been built utilising the Aire blocks. It is not known whether this was built during the war or is of post-war construction.

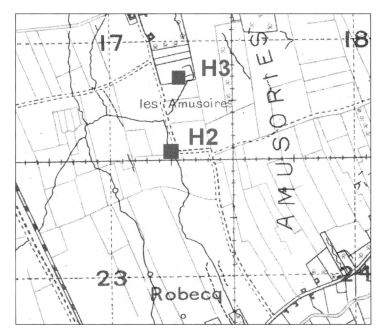

H3 Les Amusoires (50.608214, 2.565039).
Another good example, which provided mutually covering fire, is 300 yards
to the north. Both of these pill boxes were built probably by 478th/479th
Field Company RE and No.5 Field Company, Royal Monmouth Royal
Engineers, who recorded much activity around Les Amusoires during the
summer of 1918.

H4 St Floris (50.630770, 2.565168).

On the north bank of the Lys Canal near Rue des Morts (Death Road on some British trench maps), is an example of an Aire pattern pill box, which has been hit by a German shell. This had been manned by No.4 section, under Lieutenant Collinson-Jones, of 74th Machine Gun Battalion.

The rear view, with entrance, is shown below. The resulting damage shows both the strength and weakness of the system. During erection the blocks were threaded with reinforcing steel bars. Grouting with cement slurry was not carried out properly, and many, such as this one, merely have a little cement mortar on the outer joints. The steel is therefore not fully tied-in with the blocks, as can be seen in the close-up photo. However the pill box has withstood the shell impact. Some blocks have been dislodged and from the bulging line of the corner wall it is apparent that the blocks have shifted slightly. It is probable that the machine gun crew inside would have survived the explosion.

This was constructed by 250th (Tunnelling) Company RE, being one of a number built in this area. The tunnellers recorded that after construction, completion was left to the field company attached to the division, who were responsible for fitting gas curtains, ladder fixtures, fixing MG pivot mountings, any additional camouflage and clearing the field of fire of visual obstructions. The 74th MGC, who were to occupy the pill box, were also involved in the fitting-out and were shelled during this period, reporting two mules killed and four wounded.

H5, H6, H7 Le Corbie (50.644780, 2.583225).
Inside the southern tip of Bois de Nieppe, these three structures were built by 250th Tunnelling Company RE, who had recently been on a course of concrete instruction to be trained on erection methods at the Aire factory. With two built as 'machine gun emplacements' for the 5th Division, who fitted Vickers guns in two of them, and one 'artillery pill-box', they guard the approaches to the southern sector of the forest. Access is very difficult due to the broad and deep stream which fronts them but can be gained by a trek through the forest from the spine road which runs east-west through the wood.

In September 1917 the First Army established a factory to produce a pre-cast beam and block system for constructing pill boxes and bunkers in the

126

field at Aire-sur-la-Lys, with a school of instruction attached. The site was chosen because of the excellent canal and rail links for incoming materials and rail lines to the forward area. Coarse aggregate was supplied by the limestone quarries at Marquise near the coast, with sand, cement and steel contracts awarded. The making of the blocks and beams is shown in the photo below: the aggregate gauging bins, on tracks, the mixer hoppers and some finished blocks awaiting stacking. The 230th Field Company RE was given the task of commissioning and operating the factory; in the photo are several civilian employees, probably local, and some Chinese labourers.The scale of the output can be estimated by the completed blocks and beams which are in the stock yard overleaf, to be loaded onto the rail wagons for transport closer to the front, a journey of between seven and ten miles. The 250th Tunnelling Company recorded unloading blocks and beams for the pill boxes in Bois de Nieppe at Thiennes and then taking them forward by cart.

The beams incorporated steel bar reinforcement and the blocks had expanded metal for strengthening and to reduce concrete spalling inside the shelter when struck by a shell. The standard design, with a few variations, was for the block walls to be dry-laid with connecting rods and then wet cement grout to be poured down to cement all together. This was not a

successful method as the grout did not penetrate the layers: some engineers seem to have realised this and mortared the joints as the walls went up although many still existing show very poor contact between steel bar reinforcement and blocks and beams. Although not part of the original design, many had a thin layer of mortar spread to the roof to prevent rain ingress.

The total number produced at the Aire factory is not known but was probably several hundreds. The peak production period was June and July 1918 when 700 roof beams and 7,000 wall blocks were produced per day, totalling about 250 tons of reinforced concrete.

Reports were made of hits on the pill boxes by German shells[6]. One, which had been recently completed east of the forest of Nieppe, received a direct hit from a 5.9 inch howitzer shell on the centre of the roof. The report stated that the occupants may have suffered concussion but would otherwise be uninjured. The report included the following diagram to illustrate the damage.

Another report was a direct hit from a 77mm shell to a pill box which was completed 48 hours before being hit. Some minor damage occurred and one top beam was displaced but the machine gun crew were unhurt.

A Brigade HQ bunker was hit by a 5.9 inch shell and some slight roof beam damage occurred but no major cracks or breaking. Another report said that a machine gun pill box was hit on the corner of the loophole and damaged some blocks and the machine gun table pivot, one of the machine gun crew was injured but another gun was mounted immediately.

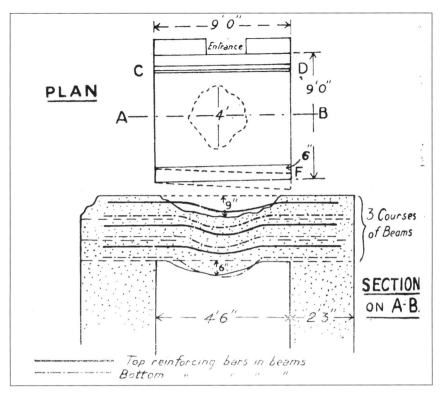

H8 Le Laurier (50.658657, 2.600584). In the Bois de Nieppe are a number of Aire pattern pill boxes in various states of condition. This one, which was occupied by a machine gun crew of 5th Machine Gun Corps, has been severely damaged by impact from a shell on the front wall. It has knocked away several layers of blocks and beams.

H9 (50.662166, 2.590284). Another one, close to the driveway which dissects the forest, shows almost total destruction from a direct hit.

H10 (50.664179, 2.590671). One close by shows some minor damage to one wall but is still in sound structural condition. This was Concrete Shelter No.3 constructed by 257th Tunnelling Company RE, who record building it next to the road through the forest, Fosse Way (Via Roma to the 5th Division).

H11 (50.665050, 2.572217). Another one in the depth of the forest marked 'The Great Oak' on British trench maps and 'Le Gros Chêne' on modern French maps, at the top of the ride or forest road named Artillery Row. (Adjacent rides were Infantry Row and Tank Row, other rides  were given names by the 5th Division who had just returned from the Italian front – Via Roma and Via Padorna, and two camps in the wood were Villorba and Spresiano.) This pill box is of a slightly different layout, being a command post rather than machine gun pill box and having had a sheltered doorway added. It shows shell damage, as can be seen on the right in the photo, where some roof beams have been blown off. The interior shows no sign of any damage and the occupants were probably unhurt except for concussion.

H12 (50.667852, 2.591701). Similar shell damage can be seen in the northernmost of the Aire pattern shelters which was on the boundary of the Second Army and built by 250th Tunnelling Company. A direct hit has been

received, and some structural damage has occurred to the front side facing the Germans, however the rest the shelter is unaffected as can be seen in the second picture. This shelter also has a thick cement layer to the roof, probably applied as a result of earlier rain penetration between the roof beams.

H13 Merville Villa (50.654440, 2.601571) Bois de Nieppe. Not all of the machine gun pill boxes in the forest constructed by 250 Tunnelling Company are of pre-cast blocks and beams. Just inside the eastern edge of the forest, near where the old railway line cuts through the trees, is a large monolithic in-situ bunker built for two machine guns for use by 5th Machine Gun Corps. Inscribed into the wet cement on the rear wall by the doorway in large letters is 'Merville Villa'. The origin of this name is a mystery as neither constructors nor machine gunners, who probably gave the name, had been in Merville, which had been taken by the Germans from the 61st Division.

Inside the doorway is a rather more poignant inscription, probably by the same hand: 'A Holden 5 MGC'. Private Alfred Holden of 5 MGC was killed here on 31st July 1918 and is buried in Tannay British Cemetery, just outside the southern edge of the wood.

133

H14 (50.655147, 2.602215). Close by, about 50 yards to the north, are the remains of a similar monolithic pill box which has been hit and severely damaged. The explosion has shattered the walls causing the thick roof to fall in. An examination shows a low level of workmanship and construction, which has given a weak structure: the concrete has been very poorly mixed and incompletely compacted, with poor joints and little steel between the walls and roof.

H15 (50.663370, 2.595595).
Adjacent to the car park and old railway halt building is a solid concrete machine gun post, built by 527th Field Company for the 40th Machine Gun Corps, that gave control over passage up the road towards the wood. Difficult to discern from the front, because of the plant and shrub growth over what was the protective earth bank, and covered in ivy and weeds at the rear, it is now used as a storage room by forest workers, with a modern steel door.

H16 (50.692252, 2.599763).

Built into the buildings of a farm close to Bois de Nieppe is a double-chambered bunker which is an unusual juxtaposition of monolithic in-situ concrete and pre-cast blocks from the Second Army concrete factory in Arques. The 211st Field Company RE recorded this work in the summer of 1918 as:

> 'left Battalion HQ (E 20c 55.10) Reinforced concrete covered shelter, large, being in progress. Reinforced concrete block pill box of which the floor is complete.'

This was later an Advanced Dressing Station attached to the 40th Division, which took over this sector after being re-constituted following disbandment after very heavy losses earlier in the year during the Battle of the Lys. In the British cemetery opposite are those treated here who unfortunately did not survive their wounds.

The Royal Engineers were proud of their handiwork and engraved a plaque with the date '22 AUG 1918' over the entrance. This was not a quiet area however; on the following day, 23 August, the 31st MGC based near the ADS reported *very considerable shelling. The Hun seems to be searching for the battery of 6" Hows that came up here and registered – about 200 8" shells were sent over in this neighbourhood'.*

The photos here show the two parts of the shelter and the inscription over the entrance in the existing barn.

The blocks and beams used in the Second Army zone, which in 1918 was from the Forest of Nieppe northwards to join the Belgian Army just north of Ypres, were produced in the Arques factory, which had been established to produce an alternative pattern to that at Aire. In this pattern the expanded metal reinforcement was omitted from the blocks and the grooving in the beams was different to allow horizontal reinforcing bars to be placed between each layer of blocks.

To compare the relative resistance and effectiveness of the two different types of structure produced at Aire and Arques, and – more importantly – to find the best features of each for development of an improved pattern, extensive trials were carried out on pill boxes shipped to and erected at Shoeburyness in Kent. The results of direct hits with 4.5 inch and 6 inch howitzers were analysed and reported; the trials were reported as successful in that in most cases damage was minor, and some recommendations for improvements were given.

A preliminary report by the Director of Engineering Stores on the comparative trials is given in full in Appendix 1. More detailed reports by engineers commented on aggregate types and relative properties, mesh reinforcement, shape and thickness and method of placing of steel reinforcing bars. Recommendations for an improved design were given and a new factory planned at Engoudsent, although the changed situation in the summer of 1918 following the German withdrawal precluded this.

H17. Rue de Besace, Roukloshille (la Rouckelooshill on modern IGN maps) (50.753835, 2.663991) Méteren.
This machine gun pill box is built to the standard design of the Second Army pattern using blocks and beams from the Arques factory. With a single aperture for a Vickers gun (the internal face has a fitting for gun feet and iron swivel) this is a very strong and protective structure for the gun crew.

HAZEBROUCK

It was constructed in summer 1918 by the Royal Engineers for the 9th Battalion, Machine Gun Corps, who recorded the *'Chief arc of direct fire: East to East South East'*. It was one of a number of pill boxes in this locality used by the 9th Division, who had a total of fifty machine guns in twenty-three positions, some of which had concrete protection like this and with some of the open or in trenches.

Section showing block and beam construction and the end result. It is indicated on the map below, with open machine-guns on either side. The marked pill box, just to the lower right of map reference X, does not exist today.

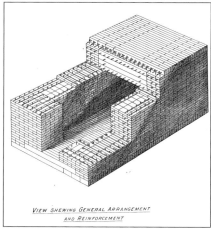

VIEW SHEWING GENERAL ARRANGEMENT AND REINFORCEMENT

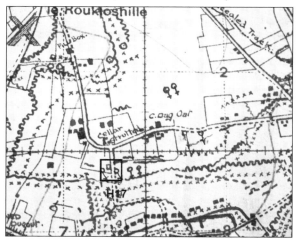

H18 In the area, but on private property, is another good example of one of the Second Army pattern precast block pill boxes, probably the best preserved on the Western Front. Constructed by 64th Field Company RE, it still retains the painted brick and mortar camouflage (the war diary records *'camouflage to Worple pill box completed'*), preserved due to a lean-to agricultural building being erected in front after the war providing protection from the weather. Also preserved are the wooden trestles with gun swivel table for the two Vickers machine guns of the 9th (Scottish) Division, which had a *'South to S.E.'* arc of direct fire. Still with the original whitewash to increase light, access is only from inside the original barn.

Side view, with rear entrance in barn and front covered by later building. Damage to the roof from a shell has been repaired with concrete blocks at a later date.

Below, left, original wooden gun trestle with Vickers gun carriage and traversing arc.

Above: Close-up of gun aperture exterior with painted brickwork camouflage.

H19 Flêtre (50.752080, 2.649518). The concrete shelter, a signals dugout, in Flêtre village was constructed by the Australians of 1st Army Troops Company under Captain Davidson. Beginning in March 1918, whilst doing much other similar work around Messines Ridge, this company made a very detailed specification for the works, including planning initial camouflage, getting materials to site, detailing reinforcement steel and gauging and mixing the concrete by hand.

The bunker, now with a crucifix on top, forms part of the boundary of a private house.

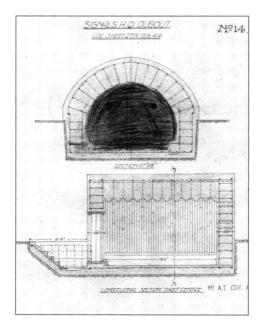

H20 Caëstre (50.750380, 2.606657).
The machine gun pill box constructed by the 3rd Canadian Tunnelling
Company in July 1918. Of a similar design to other earlier ones, such as those
at Fleurbaix, it has an inner iron shelter with a thick roof and walls of
reinforced concrete. The plans below, made by the constructors, show the
layout, a large central chamber with protective side walls and with machine
gun aperture and provision for firing the gun over the roof.

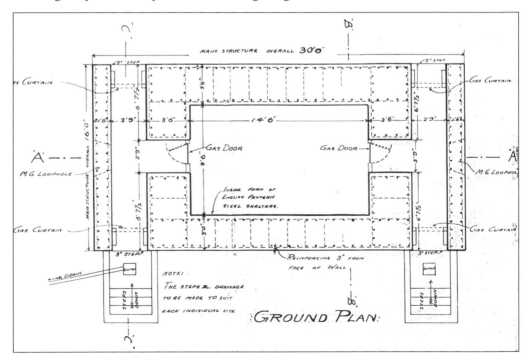

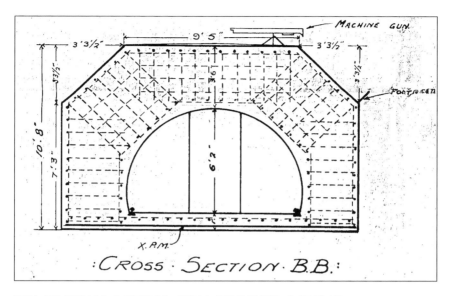

:CROSS · SECTION · B.B.:

**H21 (50.760198, 2.576846), H21A (50.760198, 2.576846),
H221B (50.764982, 2.594367) Caëstre.**

The 3rd Canadian Tunnellers also made others of the same pattern, of these three still exist to the west of Caëstre. Part of the Le Peuplier Line defences, where this met the West Hazebrouck Line, they were built as battalion and artillery HQs. Trench maps of summer 1918 show a rail spur off the main line sidings which was probably laid for the supply of construction materials and then ammunition to the batteries.

Built in the farmyard of the cluster named Instow Farm on what is today Chemin de Malin, H21 was constructed behind the existing farm buildings, which provided cover for work in progress and probably accommodation for the troops. A few hundred yards due east of H21, which can be reached down the track named Voie Communale Doorns Straat, is an identical one, H21B. This was sited behind a hedge line of trees for cover. The trees which hide the shelter today look of sufficient age to be part of the original screening. The other existing example, H21B, is in the hedge line which provided screening and camouflage bordering the paddocks between the D933 St-Sylvestre-Cappel road and the D947 to Steenvoorde. As with the other examples of this pattern they show no signs of damage having been constructed in areas subject to only light shelling in the summer of 1918.

HAZEBROUCK

H22 (50.750386, 2.606635) Caëstre.
This Moir, at Balkan Farm (Le Moulin Ghyselen on modern IGN maps), just south of Caëstre, and the remains of the one which has apparently been damaged by shellfire about 800 yards due west at Epping Farm **H22A (50.750108, 2.595702)**, were constructed on a defence line which crested the high ground in front of the village of Caëstre. This is one of the few remaining with a revolving steel protective plate. It gives a good view over land to the south and east. They were both constructed in July 1918 by the 3rd Canadian Tunnelling Company.

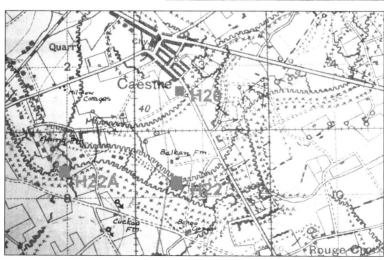

The Moir Pill Box

The Moir Pill Box was conceived and designed by Sir Edward Moir of the Ministry of Munitions. He was a prominent civil engineer who had been involved in many large projects in Britain and America. The design consisted of a series of interlocking concrete blocks with a revolving protective steel plate and machine gun mounting suspended from a steel dome cupola. It was intended for fairly quick and easy erection in the battlefield, negating the need to carry and mix concrete materials and reinforcing steel in difficult locations.

A layer of concrete was added to the roof after construction to improve resistance to shell fire. The dimensions and fittings were designed for a Vickers machine gun. The fitting was not designed to take either the Lewis or the Hotchkiss machine gun, but it was found that both could be used if fired from the shoulder with the firer leaning on the mounting. With the gun muzzle then outside the protective ring, gas fumes from the bullet propellant were not a danger.

The three photos below show the construction stages of one of the first produced to carry out trials for official approval and order for manufacture.

Extensive trials were carried out at Shoeburyness and Albert Dock to determine the resistance to impact by artillery. It was found that the design performed well when hit by 18 pound shells fired from close range. Further tests included electrically detonating 6 inch High Explosive shells buried at various distances at intervals around the pill box.

145

The photographs below show the effects of repeated explosions, first round from an 18 pound field gun, which ricocheted and burst leaving little damage, and then the result of a 6-inch shell three feet from the concrete. One third of the pill box was destroyed.

It was concluded that the design of interlocking blocks in a circular pattern gave significant resistance from shell fire comparable to in-situ reinforced structures. However as the machine gun was fired from within and the gun barrel did not extend beyond the steel ring, carbon monoxide produced when firing was a real danger to the men inside.

Further tests were carried out to find the extent of the problem and rectify it. Imperial College London was consulted to advise on levels produced and what could be permitted without harm. Trials at Albert Dock in London found that a small metal parabolic cup attached to the muzzle of the Vickers gun would project the gasses away safely. Further trials at Camiers, in France, where scientific and medical teams were based at the British military hospital, fired  1,900 rounds in 10 minutes and reported that, with the parabolic cup fitted, no ill effects were found. The early orders sent to France and constructed before work was concluded on the attachment to the Vickers gun were modified by fitting a 4 inch steel pipe through the roof for ventilation.

Earlier trials with firing from inside confined spaces, such as tanks and dug-outs, also found carbon monoxide and other gasses were produced although in these circumstances the muzzle would normally be beyond the steel, concrete or earthwork embrasure.

Following successful trials, permission had to be sought before final approval could be granted. A Moir Pill Box, with the method of camouflage as shown above, was erected in Kensington Gardens, London, for the perusal of Winston Churchill, Minister of Munitions. Churchill visited (as shown in the picture, with cigar) and examined it, asked a few questions, gave approval and then went to lunch.

Orders were placed for mass production to begin at the Royal Engineers depot factory in Richborough, Kent, and orders were placed for the steelwork. Kits consisting of blocks, steelwork, fittings, tools and camouflage were then assembled and sent to France and Belgium for erection by trained units of engineers. Most of those were destroyed or dismantled after the war, although some still exist today and can be found, such as those reported in this work, and many blocks which were surplus after the war can be found in parts of Kent. (Appendix 2)

This design found mixed favour amongst troops. The Australians were quite scathing and recorded their views; however the British did like them, and some engineers and corps found them to be extremely useful (Appendix 3) and requested as many as possible. The Canadians also liked them and their engineers constructed many, as did the Americans near Ypres. Many of those constructed by the 3rd Canadian Tunnelling Company were sited on the West Hazebrouck Line. Whilst most were built for their original use as machine gun emplacements, some were built specifically as observation posts for the artillery. **H23,** at Cassim Farm, **(50.739494, 2.542391)** is today to be found by the small road that leads behind the modern commercial centre and hypermarket. The crossroads of La Kreule is nowadays a large roundabout junction of the D916 and the N42 ring road. Minus its cupola roof, it is used for storage by the smallholder. Prior to city expansion and the commercial development it had an excellent field of view and fire.

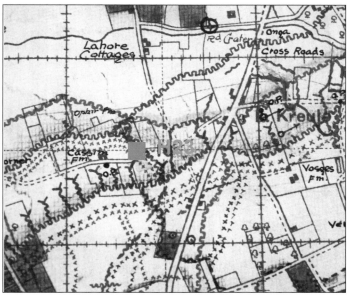

H24, H24A, H24B, H24C (private location).
This group of four Moir Pill Boxes is in a small private wood near Hazebrouck. Entry is not invited. H24, below, is in quite good condition with cupola and protective ring.

H24A. The roof supports have rusted and collapsed, causing the roof to settle on the walls. The trench leading into the pill box is still evident, full of water.

H24B. The roof is partially collapsed due to weakening by rust of the cupola supports.

H24C is still in good condition with protective ring and Vickers gun platform

H25 (50.691024, 2.493263), sited in a hedge line for concealment, was on a trench and wire defence line as part of the Le Romarin defences. This high ground was a strongpoint. The roof damage appears to be the result of a tree falling onto a roof structure with the supports weakened by rusting.

H26 (50.696981, 2.505355). Le Romarin.
This is the remains of a Moir Pill Box, which has been cut in half during a road improvement scheme, at the junction of the D138 and the original road into Morbecque (this section of road did not exist in 1914-18).

H27 (50.723240, 2.499497). This Moir Pill Box, which was until the early 2000s in a farm building which had collapsed and lay around and over it, has now been preserved by the owner of the house on whose land it now stands.

H28 (50.700902, 2.499036), H29 (50.702764, 2.496890) Le Crinchon.

To the north-west of Morbecque, by the side of the D138, are two command bunkers, a few hundred yards apart. On the south side of the road, built into the lee of the high ground, is one which is built to the standard Arques pattern No.2 but with added cover to the side entrances. This bunker shows signs of being hit by a shell on the front wall, but with little damage. It was built by 3rd Canadian Tunnelling Company in July 1918. This unit had, prior to June 1918, been working on tunnelling many mined dugouts in the area around Caëstre and Hazebrouck.

In late June three officers, four NCOs and ten ORs of the Company visited the Second Army Concrete Works at Arques for a course of instruction on erecting the pill boxes. With many structures planned, a rail siding at Caëstre was laid out in advance to receive and store all the materials – beams and blocks, sand, gravel, cement and steel – which would be required. Over the next two months they constructed a total of seventy-one concrete structures of various types. Of these, there still exist today in the area around ten Moir pill boxes, five Arques pattern block and beam structures and four monolithic concrete shelters which can definitely be attributed to them.

H29. The same pattern is to be found on the other side of the road, also constructed by the Canadian Tunnellers, with the same chamber but with slightly different protected entrance. The location, with GHQ pattern pill box H30 and command post H31 nearby, is shown on the map below.

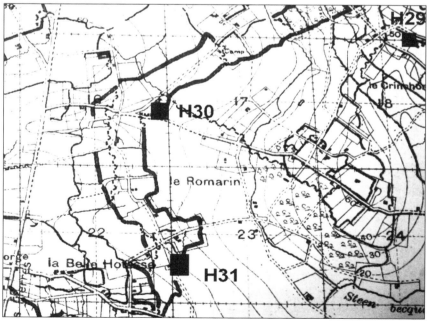

H30 La Belle Hôtesse (50.698592, 2.475207). Just to the north of the artillery shelter at La Belle Hôtesse is the sole surviving GHQ pattern pill box in this part of France, one of the few of this type to be built in this sector. It is an excellent example of the pattern, with camouflage hooks, ventilation pipes and two concrete machine gun trestles inside, just completed before the threat of another German assault was lifted by British attacks on the German line later in the summer of 1918.

One of the Royal Engineers of 173rd Tunnelling Company who carried out the construction inscribed a name plaque for posterity on the inside wall.

H31(50.688220, 2.475765) La Belle Hôtesse.
To the east of La Belle Hôtesse, looking towards Le Romarin and Morbecque, is a large concrete shelter with two rear entrances which lead off from trench level. Hidden from potential German view by the high ground and wooded areas of Bois de la Fanque and Bois de Cruysabeel, it was probably the command post for artillery.

H31A (50.724347, 2.450917).
A similar structure to this, also probably an artillery HQ, is to be found further north along the same defence system, on a line named the Sercus Switch, as it ran behind Sercus to meet the main Hazebrouck-Renescure road (N42) at Le Bonsberg. It retains the textured imprint of the sandbags which were used to act as formwork and as camouflage in a trench line.

H32 Constructed into what had been a building outside Hazebrouck on the West Hazebrouck defensive line, this Moir Pill Box has been engulfed by housing development and is now in the garden of a private house whose owner has preserved it.

H33 (50.764673, 2.469145). Another example, sited on a hedge line for concealment. This Moir has been stripped of removable parts but the main structure is intact. Marked on the map, H33 is to be found to the east of the D138 between Longue Croix and Bavinchove.

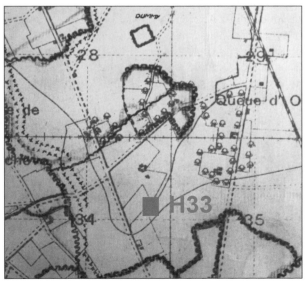

H34 (50.730255, 2.501879) was also on the West Hazebrouck Line. It stands in a field between the N42 road and the railway beside Cinq Rues British Cemetery. Without any of the moveable metal parts such as Vickers gun carriage or revolving ring, it is a good example of how extra protection was added by an outer layer of concrete. Due to the wet ground conditions it had been sited behind a built-up sandbag breastwork.

H35. This Arques pattern concrete block and beam pill box just south of the N42, near les Cinq Rues, was demolished during the writing of this work.

H36 (50.759224, 2.487717) La Longue Croix.
On the eastern edge of the railway cutting, on what had been a trench which was part of the Terdeghem Line between Wallen Cappel and Cassel (in the distance in the photo) this Arques pattern block structure was probably HQ for the battalion which was to hold the line here.

H37. This is another Arques pattern pill box which has now been demolished.

H38 (50.667552, 2.464639). West of Steenbecque, off a side-road near the junction of the D943b and the old Roman road, the D238, is a single-chambered bunker built possibly as the shelter for an ADS. It is not marked on any trench map although a building, probably a cottage, is marked here. It was constructed of an ad-hoc design of walls of pre-cast blocks and roof of beams with a steel cupola lining (a one-third section of a standard English shelter, which creates a very narrow space inside). It has an expanded steel mesh reinforcement and was probably built without any engineer's drawing using materials to hand.

H39 Pallid Farm (50.784613, 2.584657).
This was constructed for a unit of the 9th (Scottish) Division by the 3rd Canadian Tunnelling Company, who recorded on 26 July 1918 *'work commenced on concrete block dugout Arques Type 2 at* [map reference] *Q 19b 55.75'*. On the following day they were joined by a working party of 220th Transportation (Works) Company RE, who had been trained in the erection of this type of shelter at the Arques Factory.

H40 (50.769440, 2.647088).
An Arques pattern pill box for two guns, but built to a slightly different design by the 255th Tunnelling Company, with steel lintels (rail lines) over the gun embrasures. The foliage on top is continuing growth from the original placed there as camouflage.

H41 Coq de Paille (50.769091, 2.650902).
Built into the lee of the embankment of a wooded valley, Le Bois Greffier, an Arques block shelter was used in the summer of 1918 by a machine gun unit of 9th (Scottish) Division who had guns on top of the embankment.

H42 Curfew House (50.716182, 2.603588) Sec Bois.

The concrete shelter in the barn at the farmstead marked on trench maps as Curfew House was the Company HQ, right section, of the 1st Australian Machine Gun Battalion in June and July 1918. The location had been decided by Major W.R. Ffrench; it was at the southern end of the 1st Australian Division's sector, which had recently been taken over from the 31st Division.

Constructed by C Company of 1st Australian Pioneers supervised by Lieutenant R. Gregson, groundwork included preparing timber formwork, ramps for wheelbarrows, water supply and the bagging and transporting of materials from the railhead dump at Caëstre sidings. The post was later held by two guns of C Company, 104th Battalion Machine Gun Corps.

The plan with the modern photo shows how the shelter was built into the barn for concealment. The original farm buildings were largely undamaged during the war and the largest building still bears the date of building, 1883, set in the brickwork of the gable wall.

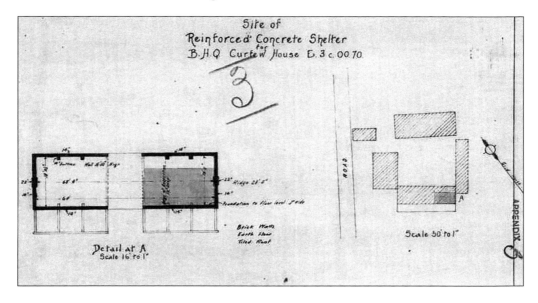

H43 (50.722484, 2.598315). As the front line settled during the summer of 1918 following the halting of the German spring advances, a strong reserve line was planned with many shell-proof machine gun positions. Major Ffrench, commanding officer of the 1st Australian Machine Gun Battalion, reconnoitred the line in early June and decided upon the best locations for machine guns *'with a view to defence by*

machine guns and suitable for construction of concrete emplacements'.

A few days later he toured the line again, with Captain Bardin of 1st Australian Pioneers, and *'visited houses selected for concrete emplacements to be constructed in them'*. Construction by A Company of the 1st Pioneers, under Major A.F. Anderson, began on several sites, one of which remains today. The War Diary records of construction refer to these variously as MG emplacements, reinforced concrete shelters and MG positions. Only in one reference is the term 'pill box' used. The pioneers were methodical in their record keeping and the bills of quantities give a total materials usage for the shelter of 119.73 tons. Most of the stone used had to be salvaged and all materials carried in bags from Caëstre, two miles away.

The photo and plan below show the general design and layout of H43, which is today partly obscured by later farm building. Another example, built to the same design at a nearby farmhouse, was demolished as recently as November 2012 as part of the Pradelles by-pass works

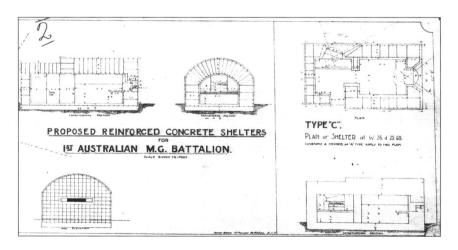

H44 Grande Marquette Farm (50.712459, 2.583847) Sec Bois.
In the yard of what was marked on trench maps as Grand Marquette Farm (the name has since been given to another farm in the vicinity) are two large shelters, both consisting of an elephant-iron core with reinforced concrete covering, and the floor of a concrete block shelter.

Sappers of 210th Field Company began work on these shelters for infantry brigades of 31st Division which were alternating in the line. Work began in July 1918, but as soon as work began the project was given to 3rd Tunnelling Company, Canadian Engineers, under Major Hibbert. Handing-over instructions from the Royal Engineers to the Canadian Tunnellers gave precise details of work to be carried out: three reinforced concrete shelters and an Arques pattern pre-cast block shelter.

These instructions included details of accommodation for the constructors, supplies and transport of materials, screening and camouflage and safe return of cement barrels. There were also instructions to obtain the concrete blocks and beams for the pre-cast shelter which were to be collected from Au Souverain RE dump on 31 July - 1 August, using five general service wagons, making two trips each night. Work was completed on 19 August after being stopped during heavy shelling for the previous days, the German artillery having been very active whilst the British were re-capturing the Outtersteene Ridge.

C Company of the 12th Norfolks, 31st Division, later established their battalion headquarters here in August 1918, alternating with other battalions of the 94th Brigade. Of the three concreted elephant-iron shelters two still exist and are in use as goat and duck housing; the floor of the pre-cast shelter exists and forms part of the base of the farm yard, used for caravan parking.

H45 Wallon Cappell (50.720648, 2.486204).
South-east of the village, hidden in dense foliage and completely covered in thick brambles next to a farmhouse on the Rue Verte, is a shelter constructed as an infantry battalion HQ. It was constructed by 3rd Tunnelling Company Canadian Engineers to an Arques Type 2 pattern. The photo shows how it appeared in the 1980s, before the brambles and shrubbery enveloped the structure.

It is shown marked as 'Bn' on the map below.

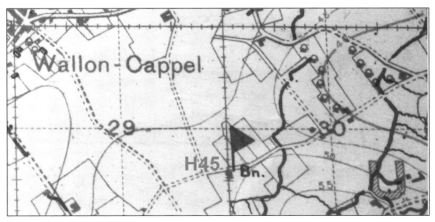

H46, Dermot House (50.716128, 2.694730) Outtersteene.

This was No.2 Casualty Clearing Station, established in mid 1917 after moving from Bailleul, and was operational until early April 1918 when the hospital was closed and moved further back to safety. The concrete chambers – five of the original six survive – are the remains of the CCS. Construction was by No.3 and No.4 sections of 8th Field Company, Australian Engineers, who started work on 2nd August 1917.

The CCS was described after an inspection visit on 21 October 1917 by the Matron-in-Chief as:

'*a most lovely position, most beautifully managed and arranged. There is a large artificial stream running through the grounds, bridges, gardens and turf plots. On one side of the stream are the administrative block and walking cases and on the other side the seriously wounded and accommodation for both medical and nursing staff. In addition to Nissen huts and marquees, they have six bomb-proof cement wards, one being devoted to the operating theatre and the remainder capable of accommodating six beds each, where during severe air raids seriously wounded patients can be safely accommodated and operations carried on without fear or danger. The nursing quarters here are quite excellent, and the Mess very good...afternoon tea was served as well as any to be had in London.*'[13]

As with the 1st Australian CCS 'Tasmania' (next entry), the 2nd CCS was evacuated before the immediate area was attacked and captured by the advancing Germans, but only after a spirited defence by 1st Queen's.

The aerial picture above shows the CCS in early 1918; the station can be identified by the road layout. Detail is difficult, but the results of shelling can be clearly seen. The location of the existing chambers is marked.

H47 Tasmania (50.720699, 2.706209) La Belle Croix.

Because of continuous heavy bombing in Bailleul the 1st ACCS (Australian Casualty Clearing Station) was relocated here in mid July 1917. No.1 and No.2 sections of the 8th Field Company Australian Engineers built the camp, consisting of Lattersby hut operating theatres, Tarrant huts, kitchen, latrines, water supply etc, with later work being carried out by 1st Army Troops Company for the 1st Australian Division. The station was christened Tasmania by the Director of Medical Services. The facilities were for 300 beds, including twenty for officers, plus accommodation for medical and nursing staff. The hospital did much work on treating mustard gas cases.

Bombing raids on the hospital continued and it was decided to construct a concrete bomb-proof shelter for the nursing sisters. This is the bunker which remains today.

The unit functioned as a corps rest camp for a period during the winter but then reverted to a CCS, receiving casualties and was particularly busy between mid March and late April 1918 as a result of the German offensive. Due to the German advancement the CCS was closed on 28 March and moved towards the rear, taking most of the huts, tents and portable items.

The raised ground on which the CCS sits, with its good views over the surrounding land, was an objective of the Germans. The 1st Queens (Royal West Surrey) and remnants of other battalions made a desperate defence but were forced back and the hospital was captured by the Germans on 12 April.

A German map dated March 1918 showing the hospital (marked LAZ, or lazaret for hospital) indicates that they knew that establishment and the 2nd CCS at Dermot House nearby, also marked LAZ, were medical establishments, but had been bombing them anyway.

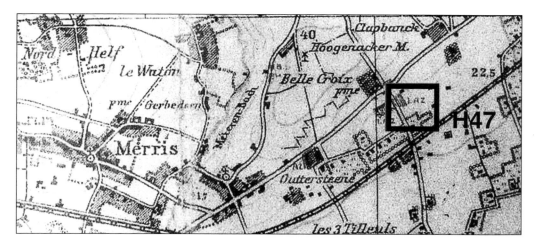

CHAPTER 7

Belgium

B1 Charing Cross Advanced Dressing Station (50.734398, 2.881551).
On entering Belgium from France on the N365 Armentières-Messines road the first village entered is Ploegsteert, with its long list of associated personages and events between 1914 and 1918. After passing through the village, on the right is Bois de Ploegsteert (Plugstreet Wood). Just before reaching the Hyde Park Corner British Cemetery, on the right can be seen the large and substantial triple bunker which replaced one which had been named originally by London troops of Aylmer Hunter Weston's 11 Brigade in 1914. Hunter Weston was to be in control of the area again a few years later when he commanded the VIII Corps which relieved the II Anzacs Corps here in late August 1917.

Constructed by New Zealand engineers as part of the planning for the forthcoming Messines offensive, this Advanced Dressing Station, described as *'three concreted nissen huts – in good shelter'*, was staffed by 11th Field Ambulance, under Major Burston of the 3rd Australian Division, in early April 1917 and was then taken over by the 9th Field Ambulance on 29th May. The 11th Field Ambulance was again at this ADS when the Messines battle was approaching. The Divisional Medical Officer planning for the Messines offensive ordered that *'The Divisional Dressing Station at Charing Cross will retain the present personnel and will be used as a line of evacuation by both New Zealand and Third Australian Division as at present'*.

The ADS was in an area with many artillery batteries and so attracted much fire from German heavy guns. During the battle the area was heavily shelled and the solid shelters, already busy with cases brought in from the various Regimental Aid Posts, protected many troops wanting shelter; the 11th FA recorded that *'A large number of slightly gassed and walking wounded cases rushed for shelter at ADS on night of 6/7th June, and rendered the work of the ADS personnel very difficult'*. Later in the day, at 4.15pm, the medical officer commanding the ADS sent a message to Divisional HQ reporting an accumulation of dead bodies which needed dealing with.

The possibility of Charing Cross and the other ADS being shelled had been foreseen by the planners and contingency plans made. The senior medical staff of 3rd Division put out on 30th May the following instruction:

'In the event of destruction of Charing Cross Advanced Dressing Station, stretcher cases will be evacuated to Underhill Farm.'

The instruction also included the possibility of Underhill Farm ADS being destroyed and the use of the Divisional Collecting Post at Touque Bertha, towards Ploegsteert village.

Although many shells fell in the area the structure seems not to have been hit and is undamaged, the original earth camouflage roof still apparent. When built the ADS was just on the edge of the wood which has since been cleared. Each doorway at the northern end of the three shelters has been blocked to leave only a window opening. The photograph below shows the ADS in use today as a fowl house; inscribed in the fresh cement on the eastern wall is a cartoon of an unknown person, possibly the officer commanding the construction.

B2 Piggeries (50.735566, 2.877356).

Through 1916 and into 1917 the farmhouse and buildings known as The Piggeries was Brigade Reserve for the units which were alternating periods here with periods in the front in Ploegsteert Wood. The 3rd Worcestershires, of 25th Division, who were alternating with the 10th Cheshires, spent much of November and December here, including Christmas Day 1916.

They were followed in January 1916 by 12th Royal Scots and other battalions of the 9th (Scottish) Division. The periods in the wood were generally relatively quiet with occasional shelling and indirect machine gun fire from both sides. However the division was not to let Christmas Day be peaceful for the Germans, so a raiding party of two officers and forty men from the 11th Cheshires carried out a raid on the Germans opposite, inflicting many casualties and making important identifications. The concrete shelter just inside the farm courtyard is typical of its type, a concreted sheet iron shelter, today holding general scrap from the farm workings.

B3 Ploegsteert village (50.737569, 2.859385).
On the western edge of the village, on the right hand side of the Rue de Romarin, this concrete shelter is marked on trench maps as being at a light rail siding, probably used to supply ammunition to the batteries situated here. The shelter, a typical construction of concrete over an iron lining, has a door opening at each end. These entrances had an additional side wall for protection. Each of these walls has been knocked over, either during the war or by later agricultural vehicles.

B3A (50.727950, 2.869087).
A similar construction is found by the road from Hill 63 to Romarin. The Canadians had established a command post here for the 4th Brigade, Canadian Field Artillery in September 1915. The present structure is a Regimental Aid Post constructed for a battalion of the 3rd Australian Division by 11th Australian Engineers and was in use in early June 1917. It was meant to have a degree of comfort and cleanliness; the quarry tiled floor is still in place. When the Battle of Messines started the RAP moved forward to Underhill Farm where the cemetery was started when the first casualties from the battle came in. This post was therefore redundant for medical purposes. There were many artillery batteries based here during the battle and afterwards and it is likely that this was taken over by one of them as a command post.

The construction, with tiled floor, is still intact but is now covered with building waste from the construction of the large modern farm storage building.

The photos below show the shelter before it was covered and the site today. The entrance can just be discerned beneath the rubble.

B4 (50.738900, 2.874298) and B5 (50.738709, 2.874448).
By the side of the track leading southwards through the woods opposite Red Lodge are two concrete shelters, one is in ruins showing obvious damage from artillery, the other slightly damaged. This latter, which retains the earth covering, is a large chamber. The two shelters were probably used by troops of the artillery batteries based in the wood and fed by the adjacent light rail siding and dump which had been named Canpac, after the Canadian Pacific line which went further west into Ploegsteert Wood. The ruins of B4, and the B5 shelter, which is often flooded, are shown below.

The map below of the western part of the wood, known as Bois de la Hutte, shows the locations of the existing shelters. The outline of the wood, as marked, is not the same as during the war in some places.

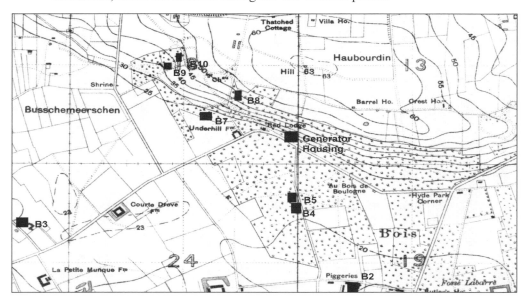

B6 Hill 63 Generator Housing (50.741289, 2.873826).

The concrete shelter between Hyde Park Corner and Red Lodge housed the electricity generator for Hill 63 dugouts and The Catacombs, the warren of dugouts which were mined into the adjacent slope of Hill 63, plus some other dugouts and electric lines going forward into Ploegsteert Wood. Prior to the opening of The Catacombs in 1916, the Canadians in 1915 had made many shelters in the southern and eastern slopes of the hill and arranged electric power in the area.

When The Catacombs were originally occupied ventilation needed to be arranged and the Australian engineers ensured that a flow of fresh air was maintained by keeping fires at some entrances to induce airflow (a mine ventilation technique which has been known for several thousand years, being used by the Romans and others). Electricity was also need for lighting and a 16hp 480 volt generator was supplied by the Australian Electrical and Mechanical Mining and Boring Company (sometimes known as 'The Alphabeticals' on account of their initials, AE&MMBC). They recorded:

'Plant was installed 28/10/16 to light extensive system of dugouts, and later to ventilate them. During the attack [the June 1917 Messines offensive] the line through the woods was cut frequently, but with the emergency line, supply was maintained.'

Improvements were made to the system from time to time which increased the need for a constant supply of electric power: the chief engineer of the 2nd Australian Division discussed this with the commanding officer of 164th Tunnelling Company in the middle of March 1918. *'Alternatives are proposed in the ventilation system, ventilation to be provided by fans drawing through filters to purify the air.'* The revision also allowed for the contingency of poison gas getting into the airways.

The concrete shelter, with its strong German-facing wall and roof with steel beams, was built to protect the generator, possibly replacing an earlier Canadian one here. The rear wall is open, to permit installation and operation of the equipment; the floor bolts and cable ducting are still apparent. The generator has been removed, probably as a piece of usable equipment, at some stage by one of the many military, industrial or agricultural organisations that would have good use of it.

B7 (50.742186, 2.869320), B8 (50.743136, 2.870908), B9 (50.744345, 2.866573), B10 (50.744671, 2.867346), Bois de la Hutte.
On the western slopes of Hill 63, in the wooded area behind Red Lodge, are the remains of several concrete shelters which are in varying conditions. The damage evident to each is testimony to the amount of shelling the area received over several years as the Germans were aware of the accommodation and operations there.

174

Just inside the edge of the wood adjacent to Underhill Farm Cemetery is the broken vestige of a shelter, B7, for medical personnel based at the Advanced Dressing Station which was at the farm there. The photograph shows how it was cast against and partly protected by sandbags. The entrance appears to have received a hit from heavy artillery which caused severe damage to the structure.

Higher up the slope in the woods is another shelter probably constructed by the Canadian engineers who established a camp here, consisting of many dug-outs. All were later used by the New Zealand, Australian and British troops who were holding the line in Plugstreet Wood and opposite Messines.

Two other similar constructions, B9 and B10, both also damaged, are found in the western extremity of the wooded area, about fifty yards apart.

B11 (50.735858, 2.890606). Ploegsteert Wood.
The machine gun emplacement which is situated down the public track through the wood, Chemin du Crampon – named Bunhill Row during the war – is one of the earliest fully intact such vestiges from the Great War. Constructed in February 1916 for a Canadian Machine Gun unit by the 11th Labour Battalion of the Royal Engineers attached to the Canadian Division, it was used by later divisions which held the wood. Strongly and solidly built, it has a wide field of fire which was directed to cover any approach through the wood along the unnamed duckboard track from the front line to Regent Street or the Strand, which were tracks into the wood from the west.

To provide sand and gravel for the concrete for this and the other pill boxes this labour battalion operated an aggregates pit near Courte Drouve Farm on the Hill 63-Romarin road, from where the material was loaded onto light rails and sent forward to near the point of usage.

Pill box B11's location is shown on the map, together with the other structures in the wood. The map shows the current outline of the wood, which in some parts is not the same as during the war.

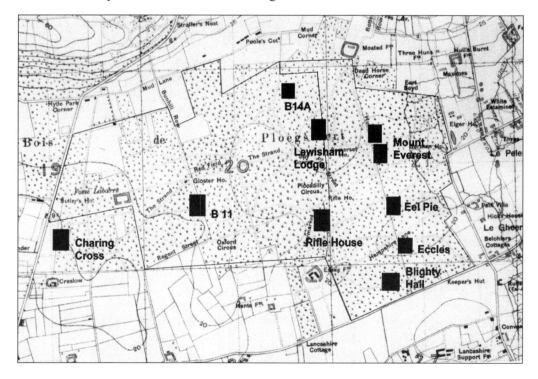

B11A Eccles Fort (50.733495, 2.905111), B11B Eel Pie Fort (50.735206, 2.904339), B11C Mount Everest (50.737976, 2.903352), B11D Mount Everest.

All are sited along the main track which had been named Hunter Avenue, probably after the commander of 11th Brigade, Aylmer Hunter Weston, which runs north-south through the wood. Alongside Hunter Avenue ran a long raised sandbag breastwork which had strongpoints or forts sited where the avenue was crossed by east-west rides through the wood. This area, which is today privately owned, is used for pheasant shooting, with watchful keepers, wire barriers and access is attempted *'sous peine de procès-verbal'*.

B11A, Eccles Fort, is a similar construction to the one at B11, sited to cover any approach along the ride named Hampshire Lane and the trench parallel to this, which was known as the Subsidiary Line.

B11B, Eel Pie Fort, protected the track along which ran a light railway named the Eel Pie Line. The front views of these are shown below.

The two adjacent pill boxes, known as Mount Everest, are shown below, (rear views). Inside each can be seen a low brick wall. Probably a later addition to prevent water entering and flooding the chamber.

BELGIUM

B12 Blighty Hall (50.731702, 2.904210).
This concrete shelter, with the inscription in the lintel over the entrance, is often visited and photographed, although nearly always flooded. A simple but well made construction of iron sheeting on two side walls, roofed with concrete, the rails on which stretchers were laid are still evident. Part of the wooden doorway lintel still exists and the walls can be seen to have been formed against sandbags which acted as some protection.

It is likely that this was a Regimental Aid Post constructed in September 1917 by 15th Field Company Royal Engineers for one of the 8th Division units which held the wood after taking over from the Australians. The Australians had previously established here a bearer relay post, which they named 'Wantage', as part of their medical evacuation scheme for the Battle of Messines. Adjacent to Blighty Hall, on the eastern side, is a depression in the ground which may have been Wantage dugout. Blighty Hall is shown below.

B13 Rifle House (50.735117, 2.900873).
The partly underground bunker near Rifle House Cemetery was built by New Zealand engineers; one of the company inscribed his name and completion date over the door. The 'NZE' and '6/4/1917' are still quite legible, as in the photo below. The name Rifle House was originally given to log huts built here by the 1st Rifle Brigade in 1914, and the name remained with Rifle House camp being used by following units. It is listed, as Rifle House RAP, as one of the Regimental Aid Posts for the Australian battalions for the opening of the attack on Messines Ridge in June 1917 and would have been very busy at the start of the battle. From here wounded were sent or taken to the ADS at Charing Cross (B1). The entrance leads to a large underground chamber which today is often flooded.

B14 Lewisham Lodge (50.738384, 2.900026).
Nearby, off the track to the north of Ploegsteert Wood Cemetery, are the broken remains of Lewisham Lodge, an unsubstantial bunker with thin walls which has not withstood the artillery shell which probably hit it. This bunker, most likely an infantry HQ, which contains much broken masonry and rubble, was probably built over a pre-existing sandbag shelter.

B14A (50.739796, 2.897773)
Near the entrance to Ploegsteert Wood (seen in the trees to the right just after turning left on entering from Mud Lane) is a partially damaged iron and concrete shelter. This is at the location of where Toronto Avenue, a duckboarded breastwork, crossed a light rail named the Prowse Boyd Line, later the Vancouver Railway, which branched into the eastern

part of the wood. The Australians established a supply dump here at the rail junction and the shelter is probably a remnant of that organisation.

B15 Prowse Point Cemetery (50.744078, 2.898467).
Inside the grounds of the cemetery can be seen the roof of the Regimental Aid Post which was used by the Australians on the opening day of the Battle of Messines and following days. A RAP, with cemetery, had existed here for over two years before the battle commenced, but as part of their planning the Australians strengthened it. The RAP was listed as consisting of one strong dressing room (which is the existing shelter), one dugout for the Regimental Medical Officer and sixteen small dugouts. Streams of wounded came through the post throughout the day, and at midnight the 10th Field Ambulance closed the post and moved further forward towards Messines. The dugout was then used as a medical facility for some time.

B16 Westhof Farm (50.736112, 2.798424).
Today known as Groot Westhof Hove, a large veterinary practice, this farm to the southwest of Nieuwkerke was an important administrative centre for much of the war. The small concrete shelter is a remnant of a much larger one which stood here. The New Zealand Division had its main Divisional HQ here, followed in turn by Australian Divisions; the 3rd opened their HQ here on 6 June 1917 for the Battle of Messines. Also based here were many of the subsidiary headquarters such as 2nd ANZAC Corps Heavy Artillery.

The corps' main dressing station, which comprised six large and twenty-two small Nissen huts and twenty-five marquees, was staffed by 9th and 77th Field Ambulance, which had fifteen medical officers and 260 assistants and around the farm were many other hutments and camps; Mahutonga and Weka

camps were nearby. The dressing station was congested on the opening day of the battle, with numerous wounded, including 300 Germans, who were treated.

Although the shelter was well in the rear of the fighting zone until the spring of 1918, it shows significant damage, probably from long range German artillery. They would have known much of the accommodation and activity here from the periods when it was captured by the Germans and then re-taken by the British.

B17 Messines South (50.758219, 2.893251).

At the location marked 'Messines South' on a map of accommodation dugouts close to the Messines Irish Memorial, is a solid concrete bunker which was a test box or telephone exchange. This connected all the communications between the front line on the other (eastern) side of the ridge with Brigade and Divisional headquarters. The structure has thick solid walls, the interior space is very small and sized for equipment and operator. It shows signs of an obvious direct hit by a German artillery shell on the rear wall; the inside reflects the damage where it can be seen that the concrete has flaked off the steel mesh reinforcement.

Probably on the site of an earlier one constructed by New Zealand engineers, it was completed by 4th Australian Pioneer Company in March 1918 when they took over this sector. It was operated by 5th Australian Signals Company, as signals point DB, before being handed over to the 19th Division. Whilst the 5th Australians were here they improved the stability of the cabling system and dug a trench to bury a cable down to the HQ in the cellars of La Hutte by Hill 63. This is marked as a dotted line on the map showing the location of the bunker, marked DB, which is the exchange number; others on the telephone system were MR, CD, LB, AV and other two letter combinations.

This buried cabling was later to have high value: the 25th Division, whose left flank lay on Messines ridge, recorded that when the Germans stormed Messines on 9th April:

'In the first stages of the battle buried routes proved to be of the greatest value. On the right sector of the Divisional front the 75th Brigade were soon out of touch with their forward station owing to its being off the buried route; on the left the 7th Brigade communications worked well during both the 10th and 11th to its battalions, through the exchange, although the enemy had overrun many of the test points behind it.'

On the inner wall of the entrance is stencilled 'ABRIS MAHIEU 1917'. The origin of this is unclear; the lettering is not of a style used by British or Australian troops and the bunker did not exist in 1917 (the location is directly forward of the German front line, with opening facing the British lines). There was a Mahieu family living at the White House near Hollebeke and a

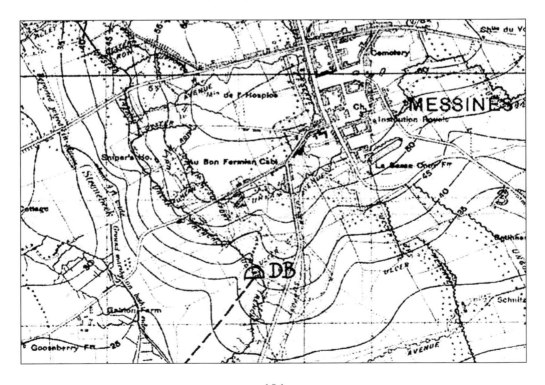

farm named Mahieu on Messines Ridge, but this is four miles away near Oostaverne.

The photographs show the entrance to a small interior and the rear wall which shows artillery impact, also the communication trench to the structure in spring 1918.

B18 Derry House (50.779478, 2.900621).

Forming part of the boundary wall of Derry House Cemetery No.2 (there is not a No.1) east of Messines is a small concrete shelter which was constructed for a field artillery battery of the 37th Division, who held this sector after relieving the 11th (Northern) Division and had established a cemetery here. The Royal Engineers of 154th Field Company, 37th Division, recorded building this shelter and others close by, with cover of three feet of reinforced concrete, between 13th and 25th July 1917. Several boot prints, set into the fresh concrete, of one of the constructors can be found on the roof.

The original farmhouse, Derry House, which gave its name to the cemetery and was apparently named by the 2nd Battalion Royal Irish Rifles, (the road on which the cemetery is located, nowadays Krommestraat, was named Antrim Road and the other farm nearby was named Ulster House) was not at the existing location but 200 yards away to the north-east. No trace exists of that building today, but it was probably where the advanced dressing station which started the military graveyard was based. The 47th Australian Infantry Battalion, followed by the 46th Battalion, had their HQ here whilst holding the line in August 1917, with their Regimental Aid Post, and buried

their casualties in the existing cemetery. During that period a long track named Dorset Street, which ran between Wytschaete and the front lines near Wambeke, snaked through the battle-scarred ground and past the post.

B19 Lettenberg (50.783090, 2.816277).

Along Lokerstraat, which runs westwards from Kemmel village, dug into the western bank of Lettenberg, a small rise to the north-east of Mont Kemmel (Kemmelberg), can be found four British concrete shelters, some of which had further tunnelled access into the hill behind. The name Lettenberg does not show on most British trench maps although it contained a hutted area known as Glasgow Camp.

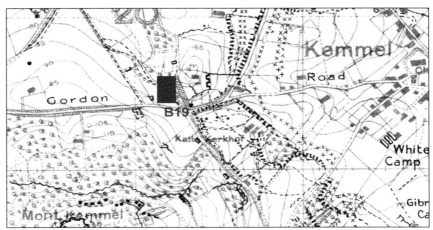

The shelters were constructed by the 175th Tunnelling Company Royal Engineers in April and May 1917, probably as part of the planning for the summer offensive, for a headquarters of a Brigade or Division of IX Corps. The Corps was to be responsible for the capture of central Messines Ridge and Wytschaete village. The shelters were later lost to the Germans who captured Kemmel
and Lettenberg in April 1918 and established a medical post here, painting a large red cross which is still visible by one of the entrances.

There were originally five constructions which were little known or visited until partly excavated and opened to the public in 2005. They are now freely open for visits although access is not permitted to all for safety and the protection of bats who have taken up residence in one.

The pictures above show the bunkers prior to renovation, and the medical post, which has since had sandbags added as retaining walls, as it would have had originally.

B20 Kemmel Shelters (50.783090, 2.816277), Locre.
To the north-west of Mont Kemmel (Kemmelberg on modern maps), on the road named Lokerstraat (known as Gordon Road to British troops) are two concrete shelters, approximately 50 yards apart. Of differing design and probably constructed by different engineers, they are the remnants of a larger group. Close by was an army camp, 'Redvers Camp', and with two railheads

– Brulooze and one nearing completion – nearby, this would have been a busy place and a likely target for German long range artillery and aerial bombing, hence the two shelters which provided protective cover.

A number of battalions were based here, such as 45th Australian Infantry, who occupied here after being relieved on the St Eloi front in early March 1918. The northernmost shows signs of damage; this, and the destruction of other shelters and dugouts in the area, is probably the result of the fighting around Kemmel in April 1918, when British and French forces were pushed off the hill and the immediate area was captured by the Germans. There were continued bombardments from both sides when the British and French tried unsuccessfully to regain the area on 26 April.

Both exhibit the use of sandbags for formwork (one still has the inner wood lining which formed the interior formwork for the concrete) and evidence of other, less durable, shelters which were adjacent. These were marked as 'Kemmel Shelters' on trench maps and were at the extent of the German advance in spring 1918, being held and used by them over the summer.

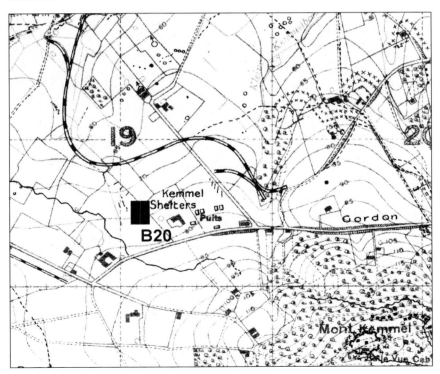

B21 Shoe Wood (50.783090, 2.816277). Klijte.
Just inside the southern edge of Shoe Wood (named as the shape resembles
a woman's shoe) and today marked Zavelaar on Belgian maps, are the
remains of three concrete shelters which are about a hundred feet apart,
usually covered in dense undergrowth and difficult to photograph. At this
point a light rail line, which connected with the main railhead at La Clytte
(Klijte), looped through the wood, with a spur outside probably supplying
the heavy artillery battery which had been here at the opening of the Messines
battle in June 1917. From April 1918, after the German advance, the front
lines came much closer to Shoe Wood and it was within range of field
artillery; it is probably during this period that two of the three shelters were
damaged. Through the summer of 1918 the wood formed part of the reserve
line, with trenches being dug in front and to the rear; it was within sight of
German observers on Kemmel Hill.

On 10 August New Yorkers of the 107th Infantry Regiment (formerly 7th NY Infantry), newly arrived in Europe, were billeted in and around Shoe Wood, accompanied by British troops as mentors to initiate them in trench warfare. They recorded that they *'discovered that warfare under these conditions contained none of the vainglorious romance they may have dreamed of...soldiering in the front line was anything but a tea and macaroon party...a sordid, smelly, sickening business'.*[14]

After two weeks of digging, stretching barbed wire, carrying water, rations and ammunition and carrying back the dead and wounded, they considered they had learnt a lot in and around Shoe Wood. The location of the shelters, which can be reached via the footpath entrance from the road to the east of the wood (Zavelaarstraat), is shown on the map below.

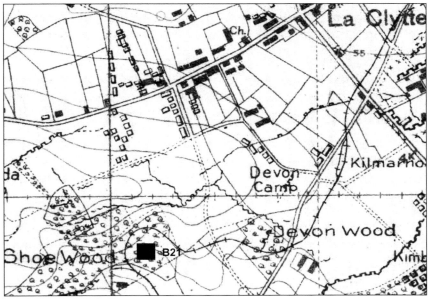

B22 Scherpenberg(50.793797, 2.780807).

Scherpenberg is a fairly steep-sided wooded hill by the N375 road between Locre (Loker) and La Clytte (Klijte). The six dugouts on the western side of the hill were home to many divisional staff for much of the war. The high promontory made a good observation point with views over the battlefront areas to the east, towards St Eloi and Wijtschate. The hill also provided cover from incoming shellfire. It was utilised by the British at a very early stage and when the line stabilised became more and more important. Permanent headquarters were constructed as well as many hutted camps. King George V visited here on 14 August 1916 during a tour of the Western Front.

The six shelters are built into the lee of the hill. They were constructed with mass concrete cast over elephant–iron forms, some of which were apparently removed in post-war years, with earth topping then a concrete burster layer and brick masonry forming the rear and front walls of some, with steps at the rear of the chambers leading up to a higher-level trench. They are all of similar construction, possibly built quite early, in 1915, making them some of the oldest surviving structures from the Great War. Some have traces of nameplates over the entrance which have been removed at some stage or weathered away.

Above ground concrete shelters were needed on these parts of the hill because the complicated geological nature of the terrain did not allow for tunnelled dug-outs all over. A double vertical geological fault line divides the hill into areas of water-bearing sandstone, in which tunnels flooded and were abandoned during works, whilst other parts of the hill comprise dry and impervious clay and dry sand in which tunnelled dugouts were possible.

There was obviously much activity here during the build-up and operations for many battles, such as the actions at St Eloi in 1915 and 1916 and the Battle of Messines in 1917, when the 16th Division had their HQ here. The hill was also a centre of activity during the winter of 1917/18 when defences were being planned against an expected German attack in spring. The 37th Division planned and organised much of their defensive work from here, handing the concrete shelters over to the 4th Australian Division who relieved them in mid January, establishing their administrative, Artillery, Medical, Signals and Engineering HQs in the shelters.

Comments by the incoming commanders, who inspected the new quarters for their staff and troops under their command, were varied. The Chief Engineer said of the field companies' accommodation: *'All the camps were excellent, and the most comfortable yet occupied'*. However the Assistant Director of Medical Services for the Division said the accommodations *'when taken over were found to be in a very bad state. This also applies to most of the stations taken over by this Division in this area. Chief points noticed were dirty drinking water storage tanks, prevalence of lice, rats, filth, absence of refuse bins, refuse pits, absence of urinals, anti fly-proof latrines. Collections of old tins and filth strewn in every direction.'*

The molen or windmill atop the hill continued working for much of the war, but it was destroyed by shell fire on 25 April 1918 as the Germans got closer. Having captured Kemmelberg and the land approaching Scherpenberg, they were brought to a halt at the foot of the hill by a mixed force of British and French troops. The action and desperate fighting to hold the hill was given the nomenclature the Battle of the Scherpenberg. The line stabilised midway between the two hills so the dugouts were much closer to the front line fighting than before and trenches and defences in the vicinity – such as Marjorie Trench, Molen Lane and Marjorie Post – were bolstered as these shelters were used by front-line troops.

The location of the dugouts, which can be difficult to find in the undergrowth, at Scherpenberg South Camp is marked on the map below.

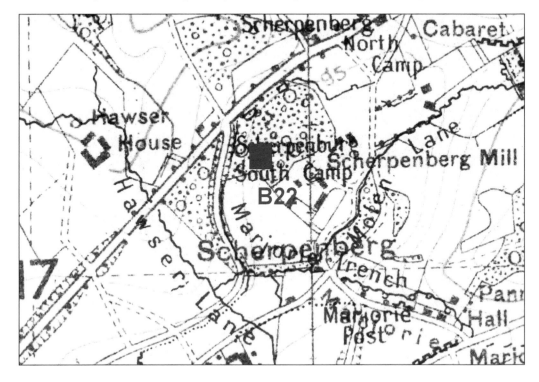

B23 Hepper House (Cambridge Siding) (50.811460, 2.803220).
Hidden and built into the cellar of a farm which was named Hepper House, is a strong and well reinforced concrete machine gun post. Prior to April 1918 and the German advance, this had been a back area, relatively safe and quiet. The immediate area was a large and active rail siding, named Cambridge Siding, with goods storage and hutted accommodation.

In expectation of a German offensive here the British set about constructing defensive positions. After the German advance was stabilised – the front lines were by now less than a mile from here – the British began to reinforce and strengthen these. It is quite likely that this machine gun post, which has ventilation via the roof, dates from that time. It was constructed by Royal Engineers (possibly of 41st Division) who by now had a good understanding of constructing and concreting structures to provide effective shell-proof protection.

The post, with the machine gun embrasure bricked up, is beneath a private farm building, which carries the date 1865 in the original brickwork.

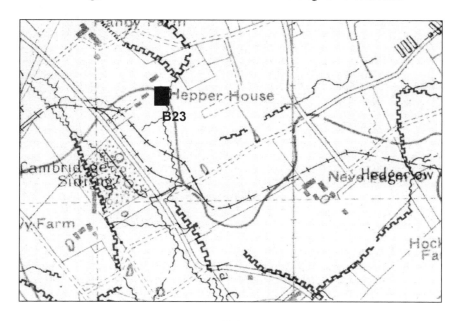

BELGIUM

B24 Hooggraaf (50.822814, 2.724878) South Poperinge.

This three-chambered bunker is situated off Brabantstraat, near where it leaves the N398 Poperinge-Westouter road. This junction was named Ogden Fork by the British and the hamlet of Hooggraaf is shown as Brabant on some maps. It is reached from the track running alongside the café on the corner, De Hertog.

The triple bunker comprises a cast in-situ central chamber, on either side of which has been constructed a bunker using concrete blocks and beams from the Second Army factory at Arques. Of substantial total size and situated next to the single line standard-gauge railway which ran from Hazebrouck to connect with metre and narrow-gauge lines further forward with ammunition and stores, it was constructed probably as a shelter for corps functions. For several years various corps had been based here at Hoograaf, from the Canadian Corps in 1916 to others in 1918.

All three have entrances at either end, being side-on to incoming artillery fire. There is also the remnant of a protective blast wall across the doorways, which was probably a later addition. This appears to have been broken, probably by an artillery hit. There is also evidence of several hits on the eastern (German facing) side of the roof but this has caused minimal damage.

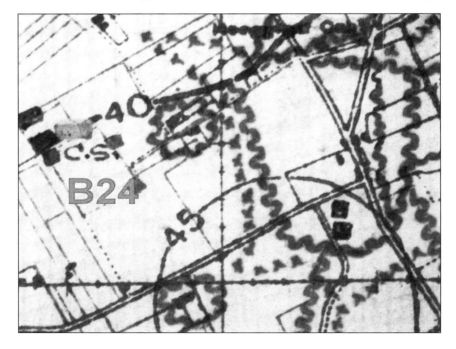

Today the bunkers are used as shelters for cattle. It is shown on the map as 'CS' for concrete shelter behind the trench strongpoints around the Hoograaf cross roads, although the rail line is not marked on this map.

B24A (50.80790, 2.83394) Hallebast.
Although not a structure in terms of defence or cover from incoming fire, the tank bridge over the Kemmelbeek, which carries the road between Hallebast and Vierstraat, illustrates that blocks and beams for pill boxes were also used for other constructions. The parapet walls of the bridge are composed of concrete blocks from the Second Army factory at Arques, as used in machine gun pill boxes.

The 245th Army Troops Company RE recorded starting work on the 'bridge for tanks' on the afternoon of 4 September 1918 and working continuously in three shifts until completion on 7 September. During the same period they were also involved in screening the roads in the vicinity from German observation. The start of the British offensive on 28 September to re-take Wytschaete and the Messines Ridge was approaching and routes which had been continuously shelled by the Germans needed maintaining and improving.

The tank bridge, possibly the only remaining one of its type, is pictured below. On the end of one parapet wall one of the constructors left an inscription '245 Cy A.T. R.E. 7 Aug 1918'. The reason for the discrepancy between war diary month, September, and inscribed month, August, is unknown.

B25 Nine Elms (50.850450, 2.691650) Poperinge.
Along the road named Helleketelweg due west out of Poperinge, inside the existing barn 500 yards west of Nine Elms Cemetery, (marked as Cemetery opposite the Hospital Cross camp on the map below), is a substantial double-chambered machine gun post. It originally had an observation post on top which was later removed by the farmer in an unsuccessful attempt to demolish the bunker. The two gun embrasures are placed to give a covering field of fire over the land to the south-east to north-east.

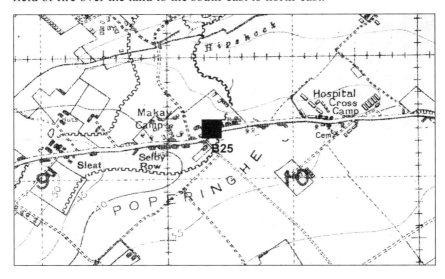

This was part of the West Poperinge Line defence system. Construction work by F Platoon of 105th US Engineers, 30th American Division, under Master Engineer Stockard, started on 11 July 1918. They spent several weeks on the concrete work, based at the adjacent Makay Camp; by mid August they reported that the work was almost complete. Completion was nearing but not achieved by 3 September, when the American engineers moved down to the Somme with their division to prepare for the attack on the Hindenburg Line at Bellicourt. They were relieved on the West Poperinge Line by Royal Engineers of the 35th Division, who decided not to carry on with the project.

The Americans had whitewashed the interior and used timber forms for the machine gun apertures; these were not removed and are still visible from the outside of the barn. They left an inscription in the concrete on the outer wall 'USA 1918'; other words were also inscribed but are not legible today.

B26 Brandhoek (50.853005, 2.781558).
This is situated in the garden of a private house on the western side of
Brandhoek, and was constructed by 105th Regiment of Engineers, 30th
American Division, in August 1918 as a part of the Brandhoek Line, also
termed the Yellow Line. This ran behind the Vlamertinge Line and in front
of the East Poperinge Line. The engineers of the 30th American Division
spent much of the summer of 1918 in this area, both in the front line and
working on rear defences such as this. On a slight rise, this simple but fairly
substantial and solid structure comprises a double chamber without gun
embrasure. It has good commanding views of the approaches from Ypres
along the road and the railway line.

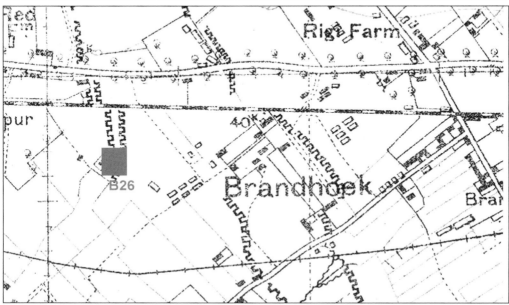

B27 Scott Farm (50.778790, 2.876272).

By the Wytschaete-Kruisstraat road (nowadays Wulvergemstraat) is the bunker which is close to the farmstead of that name, the present house being on the site of the original. The concrete shelter is built into the lee of the rising ground giving protection from German observation and artillery.

The bunker does, however, show signs of shell fire both from the east (German) side and the west (British) side, probably from when the bunker was occupied by the Germans in the summer of 1918. With a quite substantial overall size, it has a very small interior and cannot be considered an efficient use of manpower and materials for the accommodation produced. The formwork of corrugated iron is clear.

This was battalion headquarters for units of the 14th Australian Infantry Brigade whilst they were in reserve and most troops were being supplied for working parties. The 54th battalion was based here, and later the 55th battalion recorded that on 21 March 1918 they *'took over right reserve dispositions with Bn HQ at Scott Farm'*. The picture below shows that it received damage from British as well as German firepower.

B28 Hiele Farm (50.803006, 2.898717).
By the road between Oostaverne and St Eloi, the concrete dugout close to the farm given this name in the early days of the war, is a large and solid shelter constructed in late 1917 as part of the defences of the northern edge of Messines ridge. Built of concrete placed over elephant iron supports with a rear wall strengthened with concrete blocks jointed together, it originally adjoined another similar structure. This survived the war but was later destroyed, possibly during World War Two.

This was an important and busy location with a number of activities including the headquarters of the infantry battalion holding the front just over the high ground behind. Also housed here was the control centre of an artillery battery, with a line to a forward observation post and visual signalling relaying to artillery and divisional HQ further back. No.7 battery of 3rd Australian Field Battery Brigade was based here and had their guns close by. They had relieved No.12 Battery in early February and maintained harassing and targeted artillery shoots on the German positions to the east.

A battery of the Royal Horse Artillery occupied the shelter for a while and units of the 9th (Scottish) Division, who had been in this area two years previously in February 1916, but had only arrived a few days before the attack and had had little time to organise themselves and their defences. Nevertheless they held back the Germans trying to advance through the morning mist on 11 April, until forced to retire when the attackers broke through on their southern flank.

The photographs above and right show how it stood in the early 1930s, prior to partial demolition, and today.

B29 St Eloi (50.808603, 2.891631).
Behind houses which front onto the N365 Armentiersweg, about 200 yards south of the roundabout junction with the N336 Rijselsweg, is a typical semi-circular concrete shelter. It is still in very good condition with the iron formwork lining intact on the inside and with corrugated iron sheeting forms clearly evident on the exterior.

It was probably built between November 1917 and February 1918, when the village was almost totally destroyed with no above-ground accommodation, by one of the divisions – most likely the 37th or Australian – which held this sector during that period. Sited near the western bank of one of the large craters from the June 1917 mining offensive, it is on ground high enough to give good views over the land towards Warneton and the east, with the front line then about two miles away towards the Ypres-Comines railway line near Hollebeke. Today, trees obscure the view. This vantage point had made St Eloi a target for both sides and fiercely contested throughout the war. The height of the embrasure suggests that it was intended for observation over the German lines rather than for a machine gun.

The area was held by the 9th (Scottish) Division on 25 April 1918 when the Westphalians of the German Fourth Army attacked and captured this high ground and surrounding area en-route to taking Mont Kemmel. The 5th Cameron Highlanders had held on to St Eloi, making a strong defensive flank until forced to retire during the evening of 25 April. Despite the heavy fighting around it, the structure has apparently survived any localised shelling

or damage and remains intact. In 2003 the bunker – which had previously been on private land – was opened to the public with easy access, and can now be visited (on obtaining the gate code from Ypres Tourist Office), except during winter when it is closed.

The pictures (left) show how the bunker today is being overtaken by plant growth, and as it appeared in open ground earlier in the 1970s, when it was possible to appreciate the field of view it afforded over the land to the east (above).

B30, B31 Porridge (Oaten Wood) (50.803087, 2.893782).

The small copse on the right of the N365 from Wijtschate to St Elooi, in the lee of the ground rising to the east, was in late 1917 and 1918 the terminus, named Porridge, of a rail line constructed to supply ammunition for the batteries behind and in front of the higher ground. Two concrete shelters were constructed in the wood, most likely to provide cover for the troops working at the terminus. Both of these have been hit by artillery fire on the eastern sides suggesting German hits. Also in the copse can be seen the remains of a collapsed dugout, which had been tunnelled into the ground. They were probably built by Australian troops who were very active here in the winter of 1917/18.

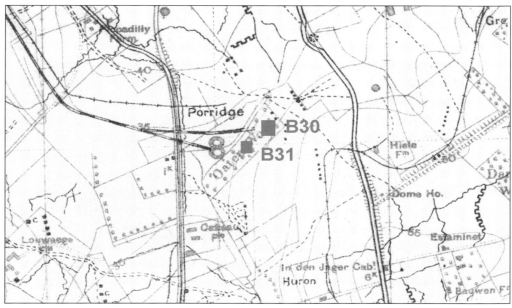

B32 The Bluff (50.815206, 2.915524) (Palingbeek).
In the trees and undergrowth just beneath the track which leads from the Palingbeek café, largely covered by forest debris, is a bunker which marks the British front line where The Wynde trench looped down towards the canal, at point I.34.1, before the battle of Messines in June 1917. The Bluff – spoil from the canal cutting – had been stoutly defended since early in the war as the British were intent on keeping this high ground. The Germans were equally keen to capture what they called Die Grosse Bastion: both sides had been engaged in mining and counter-mining and the surrounding slopes were mazes of tunnels and dugouts.

The existing shelter – a typical British design of concrete over corrugated iron, which probably connected to one of the many tunnels – is likely to date from the period in early 1917 when the 47th (London) Division, who had been here since October 1916 when they took over from the 1st Australian Division, were making preparations for the forthcoming battle and establishing infantry, medical, machine gun and artillery command centres. Royal Engineers attached to the division were very active and did much work on solid constructions.

During the winter of 1917/18 the Australians held this sector and it is probable that the shelter, now beside a communication track named Staffords Walk, was again used. The 2nd Australian Field Company recorded re-fitting as many shelters as possible to provide accommodation for troops. This included many of the German shelters, several of which still exist in various states of repair, further east along the canal bank.

During the summer of 1918 The Bluff was in German hands and a British intelligence map shows that the shelter, and others which existed around, was being used by the Germans for accommodation.

B33 Lock 7, King's Way (50.820239, 2.895885).
King's Way was the name of the pathway, today named Bijlanderpad, along the northern bank of the canal between the N336 and the by-road which crosses the canal at Spoilbank Cemetery. Today most of the canal and adjacent banks are overgrown and difficult to access. Part way along are the remains of one of the canal locks, No.7. The stout walls of the lock gave some protection from shelling and later several shelters, the remains of which are still evident, were constructed here. In March 1917 520th Field Company RE (formerly 2/3rd London Field Company) of 47th Division, *'took on work on the spacious concrete dugouts at Lock 7, and moved into them as soon as they were completed. The work here was subsequently finished by 518 Field Company, and the dugouts were used during the Messines battle as an artillery group headquarters'* [10]. These shelters, which were designed and constructed to be shell-proof, were later used by a number of units as headquarters.

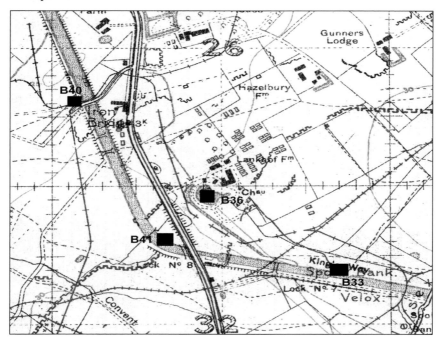

BELGIUM

On 25 February 1918 the 2nd Field Artillery Brigade of 1st Australian Division established their HQ in these shelters, with four gun batteries close by. The HQ was in direct communication with their OP, which had been opened in the existing OP at Hill 60.

The photographs below show the condition of the lock in August 1917, and the interior of the least damaged bunker, which consists of a concrete chamber built during the winter of 1917/18. Adjacent are the remains of another shelter which appears to have received a direct hit from a heavy artillery shell. The walls and steps down into the chamber are still evident.

The map shows the location of the Lock 7 shelters and others in the vicinity.

B34 Transport Farm (50.836361, 2.902483).
This standard bunker, which stands in the field behind the restaurant De Steenen Haene on Komenesweg, is a good example of a typical British construction, being several feet of concrete reinforced with expanded steel mesh, with some steel pickets, placed over an elephant-iron lining on the interior. Steps lead down into the chamber. The rear wall, which faced the German lines, is up to three feet thick, with the front wall with doorway about 1 foot thick. On the exterior are impressions of sandbags which were used both to form the outer concrete and to act as extra thickness for explosion resistance.

The bunker is located at what was the junction, named C2, of two light rail lines which connected with the front fighting line and a spur to Zillebeke Lake Sidings. It is very close to Railway Dugouts Burial Ground (Transport Farm), which is over the road

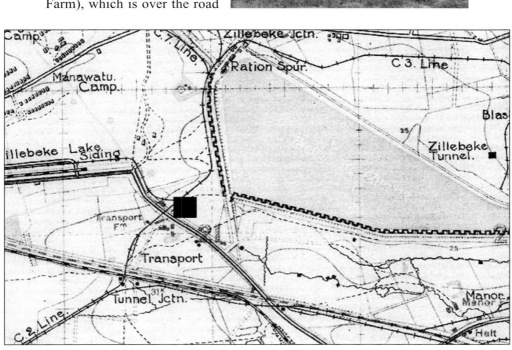

and it is likely that this shelter was an off-loading point for wounded being brought by light rail to the Advanced Dressing Station at Transport Farm.

B35 Onraet Farm (50.794238, 2.886819).
The concrete shelter here was built by 153rd Company Royal Engineers, of 37th Division, commencing on 9 August 1917, for use as Brigade HQ, into the original farmhouse that stood here (still evident) and re-using what had been a German command post named KTK (*Kampf Truppen Kommandeur*, or commander of front-line troops) Grenze. This had been fortified with shell-proof cover which the engineers strengthened with reinforced concrete, with a different opening direction away from incoming artillery.

The concrete structure still contains some of the brickwork of the farmhouse (the hearth and chimney were incorporated into the concrete and are still evident) and some German corrugated iron probably recycled by the REs. To prevent rainwater entering the HQ a lining of tar was applied to the ceiling and this can still be seen. This was probably a part of the refurbishment carried out by 14th Australian Field Company in January 1918 in preparation for the establishment of the defensive system.

Several Australian battalions had their HQ here during the winter of 1917/18 whilst providing working parties for front line duties: the 56th Battalion recorded receiving 400 pairs of clean socks here in March and issuing them to troops in exchange for dirty and wet socks. They were later relieved by the 7th Battalion who had their HQ here. The shelter was also a

stretcher relay bearer post used by the Australian medical services. Many troops of the battalions were quartered in dugouts and German concrete shelters still standing in the adjacent wood.

B36 Lankhof (sometimes Langhof) Farm (50.822590, 2.890826).
This group of buildings, situated by the N336 Rijselseweg south of Ypres and containing seven bunkers dating from 1917/18, was originally sited within the moated area. Throughout the early years of the war the British based units here. The farm came into prominence when the 47th (London) Division sited artillery here for bombardments of the Germans prior to the opening of the Messines offensive and for the defence of Hill 60 when the 23rd Division were beating off a German onslaught there on 23 April 1918.

Later in 1917, when the Passchendaele offensive was closing and it was clear a defensive strategy was needed for the coming winter, it was decided to construct shell-proof accommodation here and Royal Engineers of 153 Field Company, under Major P. Moreton, began work in November, firstly putting in a rail line and siding to cater for the engineering materials that were needed. They worked on this until units of the 4th Australian Division took over the sector and their 4th Field Company, under Major Tolley, continued the work on the concrete shelters. There was much physical labour involved and the engineers were given a permanent working party attachment of seventy-five other ranks from 13 Infantry Brigade.

On 9 April 1918 the British withdrew from most of the area they had captured the previous summer to shorten the line in anticipation of a German attack. The new front line was then only a few hundred yards to the east of Lankhof so the bunkers took on more importance as a strongpoint. On 25 April a party of C Company, 6th Leicesters were almost surrounded here by 250 Germans and forced to retire and leave the bunkers to the Germans. A counter-attack was made by 8th Leicesters to re-capture them but this was unsuccessful and the Germans remained in possession for the summer but did not advance much further and so the front remained close by. A raid to try and recapture the farm, by 2nd York and Lancasters, was carried out on 5 June. Three officers and sixty-eight men carried out the attack but were beaten off by the Germans.

On the morning of 1 September an attack on Lankhof was made by the 120th Infantry of 30th American Division. The fighting for the farm took all day, with Colonel Metts, commanding the infantry, assuring Divisional HQ that it was surrounded and would be taken by dusk, which it was. They recorded:

BELGIUM

'The principal objective was Lankhof Farm, a strongly fortified forward position surrounded by a moat. The fighting was very bitter, but, with the co-operation of the artillery, who maintained close liaison with the commanding officer of the battalion, the new line was taken and consolidated.'[15]

The farm and shelters then remained on the front line for some time, until the British pushed forward later in September.

The seven bunkers are still in very good condition with little serious damage, bearing in mind the artillery bombardments and fighting which went on, in and around them. Most of them still contain features which are quite unusual and rare in British constructions – inside are the fireplaces, with tiled hearths and fire grates, probably taken from local houses, which were installed for the winter comfort of the inhabitants. See picture inset for an example.

B37 Zillebeke South (50.834978, 2.911913).
In a small copse near the southern bank of Zillebeke lake, this British concrete bunker dates possibly from before the British offensive in summer 1917. Although it only appears on British maps after the area was captured by the Germans in the spring of 1918, a shelter here is marked on German maps of June 1917. There are no records of its construction or use, although from its

location it is likely to have been a command post for an artillery battery. It is a very simple structure, about two feet of poor quality concrete reinforced with available iron and chicken wire over an elephant-iron lining, open at the rear (probably sandbagged) with two chimney vents to the front. Sandbagged impressions in the concrete are evident, suggesting that there were adjacent less strong shelters.

The track along the Zillebekevijverdreef, or Zillebeke access road, which nears the bunker (on private land), was known as The Promenade to British troops, and the embankment was a trench line with this name.

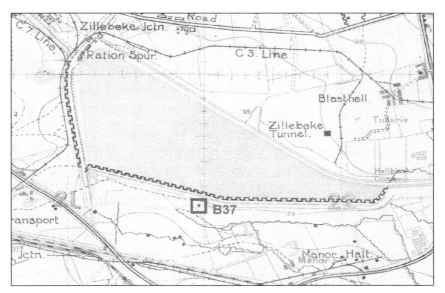

BELGIUM

B38 Voormezeele (50.817149, 2.872447).
Built into a small embankment with a ditch on the western edge of Voormezeele, (on Abdijmolenstraat) close to Voormezeele Enclosures 1 and 2 Cemetery, can be found the remains of two concrete bunkers. Both are of similar construction internally, being concrete cast over elephant-steel linings, leading into a larger chamber beneath the embankment, but were possibly constructed by different troops as the exteriors vary. Neither appears to be very strong or likely to resist the impact of a direct shell hit. In the fields immediately opposite was a large rail siding named Elzenwalle Sidings, this would have been a very busy area for much of the war.

The 4th Australian Division had a number of operations, such as the Divisional Ammunition Officer and the Divisional Salvage Officer, based here in January 1918, and the 12th Infantry Brigade record supplying infantry working parties here loading ammunition onto the light railway. Maps of March 1918, when the village was well behind the British lines, show a row of seven shelters in a line here, with the light railway connected to the main sidings, dissecting them. This light rail was also used to transport wounded from the front to the Field Ambulance adjacent.

The bunkers were captured by the Germans on 26/27 April 1917. Maps of August 1918, with the front line only a few hundred yards away, show

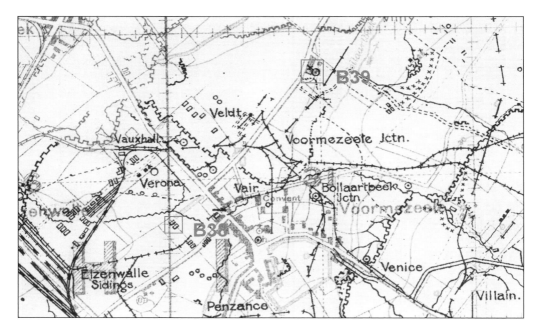

only the two existing and two others, now gone, closer to the road, so some had been destroyed during the fighting. At the end of August the village and the two bunkers were recaptured by the 30th American Division. Following their advance the American troops were not allowed to enter the bunkers in case they had been booby-trapped, and the American engineers called on Lieutenant Johnston of the Royal Engineers to advise them in searching and checking for hidden traps.

B39 Voormezeele (50.821504, 2.877817).
North-east of the village, on the road named Wittenhuisstrat, is another British bunker which shows signs of artillery damage.

The Germans took this farm on 25 April 1918, but did not proceed much further and so this was almost on the front line for the summer. Trench maps of that period show that the Germans established a forward machine gun position here. It was wrested back from them by the Americans of 119 Infantry Regiment on 31 August.

214

B40 Iron Bridge (50.825115, 2.885848).
Tucked into the embankment formed by the canal cutting and the raised ground leading to the bridge, which nowadays carries Kallepustraat to meet Bijlanderpad on the west bank, are the remains of a concrete shelter which shows obvious signs of artillery damage, with the roof destroyed. Originally a light bridge which connected Bedford House chateau with the farmland on the west of the canal, the bridge became an important part of the supply line, with several light rail lines converging here to cross the canal, and a siding named the V9 Line for artillery ammunition supplies. The shelter was most probably built before summer 1917, to protect the Foreway Engineers who had the task of maintaining the bridge and rail lines, which were subject to German artillery.

During 25 and 26 April 1918 (the Second Battle of Kemmel), units of 21st Division made a determined stand here to prevent further German progress in their advance, and this bridge and bunker marked the British front line throughout that summer until 1 September when the British, with the Americans to their right, began pushing the Germans back eastwards.

Today the re-built bridge is used by cyclists and light local traffic.

B41 Lock 8 (50.821665, 2.888069).
Dug into the slight embankment formed where the N365 crosses over the canal just south of Lankhof Farm, usually well covered and screened by coarse grasses and brambles in the north-west quadrant, is a small shelter which for a time marked the British front line. It is likely that the shelter had been there for some time; with the bridge being an important point for British traffic it was a constant target for German

artillery and by 1918, the original bridge having been destroyed, it was replaced by the Royal Engineers.

The first months of 1918 saw Australian units holding this sector and Lock 8 shelter was home to 12th Australian Infantry Brigade. On 25 April 1918 a composite battalion of 16th and 17th Manchesters, having been pushed back by the attacking Germans from the Spoil Bank, took a stand here. For three days they held this, during several heavy German artillery barrages; on the morning of 28 April the remnants of the battalion – three officers and twelve men – withdrew to join the Leicesters a little north up the canal.

B42 Hommelhofstraat, (50.841784, 2.877927) Ypres.
The street of this name follows the canal embankment as far as the site of the turning basin which is now filled in. There it bears left and at this point is a shelter which has been covered in shrubbery for many years but has since been cleared and opened. At the point of the turning basin a military track, Warrington Road, crossed the canal and it is likely that engineers were kept close by to continually repair the

bridge after shelling; this shelter was most likely constructed for that workforce.

B43 Palingbeek (White Chateau) (50.809596, 2.918442).
After capturing the large country house, owned by the Mahieu family, early in the war, the Germans had fortified it and made it a forward command

centre, on their third (reserve) line named Oak Reserve by the British. By the build-up to the Battle of Messines it had been shelled for over two years and was by now a heap of ruins beneath which were German dugouts and fortified cellars.

The heap of ruins was wrested from the German defenders at the opening of the battle by 6th London Regiment, 47th Division, after some fierce fighting, and Royal Engineers of 520 Field Company set to and organised an infantry headquarters in what was left of the ruins. This was subsequently occupied by the 11th Royal West Kents.

During the winter of 1917/18 the Australians were holding this sector and began strengthening the line in expectation of a German attack in the spring. This work included the provision of improved observation for artillery over the Germans who had their front line a mile to the east and to protect their own front in the event of attack. The Chief Engineer of the 4th Australian Division allotted the task of building the observation post to the 4th Field Company, who worked on it between 1 and 26 February. Utilising the foundations of the original chateau as a base, and with a thick covering of rubble from the ruins to camouflage and provide extra thickness, they constructed a strong and solid reinforced concrete post, with a front wall of four feet thickness, which was proof against a heavy artillery shell.

The chateau was in the front line in April 1918 when the Germans began pressing for the position, the 12th Royal Scots here came under heavy German artillery fire on 10 April and suffered many casualties before being relieved.

The OP is today on private property, in a small copse in the middle of Palingbeek golf course and access is private.

B44 Palingbeek (small shelter) (50.809650, 2.915878).

Also in the private grounds of Palingbeek golf course, but next to the small road, Palingbeekstraat, which bisects the course, is another observation post probably also made by the Australians. It comprises German concrete blocks made in their factory at Wervik and designed to be threaded with reinforcing bars. The blocks were probably there as part of the original German trench mortar position, which had been built on the site of a small pre-war kiln, so the Germans named it Backofen. The trench mortar was known to the British and had been named Arthur (other trench mortar positions nearby were Alfred, Archie, Austin and Angus) before the attack on their trench line which ran along Palingbeekstraat.

Australians of the 1st Division took over from the 4th Division and held this sector in March 1918 continuing to bolster the defences. It was probably the 2nd Field Company who decided to re-use the German concrete blocks

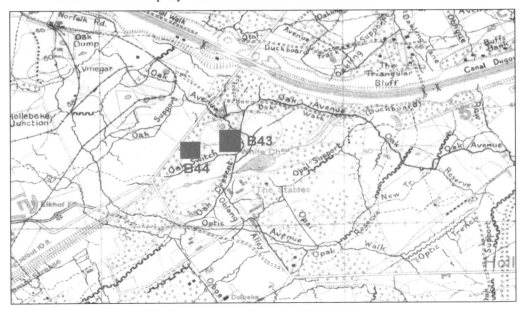

which they found here and construct the shelter which gave a view towards the front line. They recorded working on a number of *'miscellaneous strong points at White Chateau'* before being relieved by British troops.

The 11th Royal Scots, 9th (Scottish) Division, held this shelter and White Chateau, holding off determined German attacks on 10 and 11 April, with a withdrawal to the south when this became a flank defensive post, until taken by the Germans. The photograph below, with the German lines away to the right, shows the rather irregular way in which the blocks have been used. A side wall of cement mortar offers a small degree of protection to those entering the OP from the rear side, with the broken remains of the original German bunker to the right. The other photo (inset) illustrates how the post was for many years before it was cleared during the golf course construction.

B45 Hill 60 (50.823959, 2.929761).
Probably one of the most visited and famous Great War sites in Belgium, the spoil bank resulting from the rail cutting bears witness to some of the most prolonged fighting of the war, having changed hands many times. A number of VCs and other awards were won on and around the hill, with many brave deeds from both sides in the fights for the mound. Each side made use of the high vantage point and left their mark, from the numerous craters to the number of ruined concrete constructions.

Württembergers of the 413th and 220th (Reserve) Regiments, 204th German Division, were in possession on 7 June 1917 and their engineers and pioneers – probably 204th Pioneer Battalion and 116th Pioneer Company – built a strongpoint with concrete shelters and machine gun posts. When the mine laid beneath the hill was detonated and devastated the position, the *'heavy concrete shelters rocked...the effect was overpowering and crushing'* and infantrymen of the West Yorkshires, 23rd Division, cleared the bunkers which had not been destroyed. The bunker beneath the existing observation post was one of these and made a convenient base and lower chamber for the new construction. This was begun in January 1918 by the 4th Field Company of the 4th Australian Division who held the line here for the winter months.

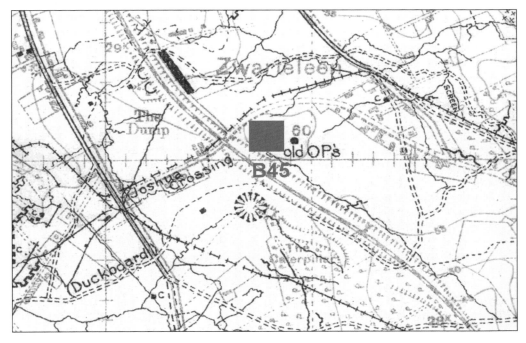

Giving good views over the front lines and German-held territory behind, it was an important position and much effort was put into making it strong and durable. The 2nd Australian Field Artillery Brigade used the observation post to watch for SOS flares from the front line, to spot and pin-point enemy artillery flashes, and to direct artillery fire on German targets in the area between Zillebeke and Gheluvelt. The OP was in direct contact with the artillery group HQ in the concrete shelters at Lock 7, it was also utilised by the Australian machine gun companies – 1st, 4th, 13th and 24th AMGCs – who had machine guns placed at locations on and around Hill 60. However the German onslaught of 15-16 April was unstoppable and the British retired from the hill, leaving it to the Germans. The drawing below shows the existing post and the original lower German chamber which is still clearly evident beneath the Australian work.

After the war Hill 60 became a tourist attraction, with a museum which included some of the underground tunnels, and several units that had served there erected memorials to their comrades. The land was purchased by an

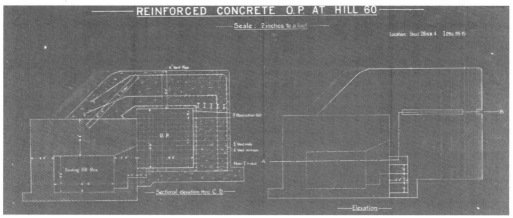

Australian brewer, John Calder, who later ceded it to the care of the Commonwealth War Graves Commission.

There are remains of other German and Australian concrete shelters on Hill 60 but none are as intact as the observation post. The map below, dated from when the hill was in German hands, shows the post marked as 'old OP'.

The photograph above shows the observation post shortly after the war; the ground level, which had been raised using spoil from the excavation, has since subsided to a lower level.

B46 Ravine Wood (50.823153, 2.920089) Verbrandenmolen.

Ravine Wood (properly known nowadays as Molenbos) was just behind the front line until August 1917 and became an important centre for troops holding the line here with numerous dugouts and shelters in the wood. On the eastern fringe of the wood, at the location named Calgary after the dump by the light rail which ran past here, is the remnant of a tunnel heading – which may be a tunnelled machine gun emplacement – dug into the bank. It is not known who worked the tunnel, although Canadian tunnellers were very active in this area in 1916.

The wood was given up to the Germans in April 1918, when the British retired to form a new front line about one mile to the west. It is likely that with this tunnel being so close and potentially usable by the Germans, the British would have destroyed it, leaving the remains of the entrance heading.

It is unlikely that the heading was intended to be directly shell-proof. It comprises loose rocks and roof tiles probably salvaged from the houses at the nearby hamlet, Verbrandenmolen, loosely cemented together and was probably more of a retaining wall as the structural integrity is very low.

B47 Assam Farm (De Roo Bailie) (50.836981, 2.833571).
This machine gun emplacement, situated on Groenejagerstraat which runs
north from the N375 at Dikkebus, is one of several which were constructed
in August 1918 by the 30th American Division after they relieved the 33rd
Division here as their first experience of holding a front line sector without
the supervision of a British command. Work at Assam Farm shelter had been
started by 222nd Field Company RE in July, later ten men of Company C of
the 105th Regiment of Engineers worked through August and record using
fourteen sheets of corrugated iron in the construction, the moulding of which
is still quite evident.

Two Moir Pill Boxes were also built alongside but these have since
disappeared. The Americans gave this strongpoint, which formed part of the
Dickebusch Line, the name of Fort Baird, probably named after Brigadier-
General Baird who commanded 100 Brigade, 33rd Division. He had
mentored the Americans of the 119th (2nd North Carolina Infantry) and 120th
Infantry (3rd North Carolina Infantry), who established headquarters here
while they held the front line. The emplacement was visited by Colonel
Joseph Hyde Pratt, who commanded the 105th Engineers, and recorded that

the barn in which the machine gun emplacement was sited had been hit by a German shell and burned down although the concrete shelter was untouched.

The shelter was constructed with a doorway at each end, which is unusual. At some stage, possibly after the Americans handed the sector back to the British, the doorway facing towards the front was partly blocked to leave an aperture for machine gun. The rear door is also rather wider than is normal.

The existing farmhouse, about seventy yards from its original location, dates from post-war reconstruction, with 1923 clearly legible in the gable wall brickwork.

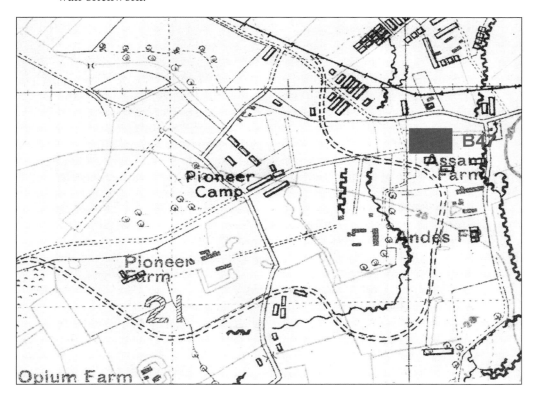

B48 (50.837482, 2.855748), B49 (50.836828, 2.854900), Belgian Chateau (Carmelite convent).

The present Carmelite convent, situated on Marshofstraat to the west of Ypres town, was the home of a local dignitary before the war. The house was named Belgian Chateau by the British with the adjacent light rail depot named Halifax. British troops occupied the chateau which, until spring 1918, was quite a way behind the lines for most of the war. After the German spring offensive the front lines became much closer and the chateau became a more dangerous place. At some stage two concrete shelters, based on typical concrete over elephant-iron lining with sandbag concrete impression side walls, were constructed and these remain in the grounds today.

The smaller of the two shelters, which has a fairly thin roof and masonry brick end wall, was constructed on the west side of the chateau building and would have had some protection from incoming artillery. The larger of the two, which is behind the wall of the access road, is more solid, with signs of the roof having had secondary protection.

The ruins of the chateau were taken over in the early 1920s by the Carmelite Sisters who rebuilt the accommodation and have retained the two bunkers (pictured above) as storage for garden tools.

B50 Bibge Cottage, Machine Gun Farm (50.858972, 2.851360).

In the barn of a private farm just off the N38 Norderring road, where it is joined by Adriaansensweg, is a large and solid bunker. The location was a busy area throughout the war with many rail sidings and a rail depot known as Machine Gun Farm. The farmhouse had been a casualty clearing station for several years, but when the defences were strengthened after the 1918 German spring attacks the area was re-organised and a brigade of the 49th Division was allocated Bibge Cottage as their HQ, followed by 41st Division who were manning the Brielen Defence Line.

The 57th and 456th Field Companies RE carried out works to make it shell-proof, with thick reinforced concrete walls and roof, built inside the existing buildings. They were assisted by five men of the 105th American Engineers who had been attached to them for instruction. As the barn remained largely untouched by shelling the construction today gives a good idea of how it appeared during the war. The concrete shelter is now used for the barn's original purpose, to house cattle; the only exterior signs of anything inside are the steel beams which jut out of the

brick walls. The photos show the farm buildings and the upper part of the concrete bunker within.

B51 (50.858972, 2.851360), B52 (50.847221, 2.880161), Ypres Ramparts.
On the ramparts of the town walls, overlooking the Dikkebuss road entrance to the town, are two Moir Pill Boxes (see section on Moir Pill Boxes for information on how these were constructed). These were placed for machine guns to defend against any approach to the town from the south; the Germans were at that stage in possession of the land between Ypres and Dikkebuss, at Voormezeele and Kemmel, with the front within sight.

Immediately behind the two pill boxes was the powder magazine for the town infantry barracks; this ammunition store, which had been built in 1817 on the site of an earlier powder store, was used by the British and survived the constant shelling of the town, being refurbished in 1998. Royal Engineers of 208th and 57th Field Companies worked on these pill boxes in early August 1918 with the assistance of four men from 105th Regiment, American

Engineers, who had been attached to the REs for instruction and training in defence works. The work was carried out at night as the ramparts were in view of the Germans who were watching for any new construction.

When the rampart walls and brick parapets were repaired during post-war restoration the two Moir Pill Boxes were retained, minus their Vickers guns, although it was thought for many years that these were merely observation posts. Small plaques stating this were attached until archive research at Kew Public Record Office (National Archives) corrected the information.

The two photographs below show the pill boxes which can be reached by the public path along the rampart walls.

B53 Anzac Camp, (50.826074, 2.863934) Kruisstraathoek.
Situated in a field to the north of Ruusschaartstraat which connects the N331 and N375, about a mile north-west of Voormezeele in what was a large army camp named Anzac Camp, are two rounded shelters showing the typical shape of British construction: a layer of reinforced concrete over elephant-iron lining. The reinforcement consists of both iron bars and expanded metal, which was found to be effective in holding concrete together when struck by artillery, reducing fragments which injured or killed the occupants. One of the shelters shows signs of being hit but with minimal damage.

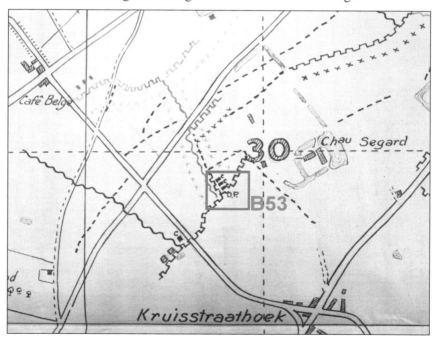

Maps of early 1918 show five huts in a line here, probably Nissen or a similar type. In late June 1918 and into July the 222nd (Tottenham) Field Engineers, building shell and bomb proof shelters for 156 Brigade Royal Artillery of 33rd Division, made three in a row with an artillery OP in front. This was by now close to the front line, and being on a slight rise named Anzac Ridge with views towards the German front lines, the area and the artillery batteries were heavily defended. Anzac Avenue trench ran just in front of the shelters with Domino Trench behind.

It was probably during September when the American troops of 118th, 119th and 120th Regiments held this area, while being mentored by 33rd Division and probably occupying one of the shelters, that the shell damage occurred. The 1st Battalion of 105th US Engineers recorded the *'reclamation of three 5.9" proof shelters'* here.

The map left shows the general location of the bunkers, near Kruisstraathoek, and the engineers' record of their work marked 'C'. A similar construction was across the road to the south-west but does not exist today.

B54 Swan Chateau Wood (50.826074, 2.863934).
By a track in the public part of what was Swan Chateau Wood – today a public recreational amenity named Tortelbos – is the remnant of a machine gun pill box showing obvious signs of artillery damage. It was not a strong construction; the walls are relatively thin and the roof has been blown off, although the basic shape and layout are still apparent. Constructed probably

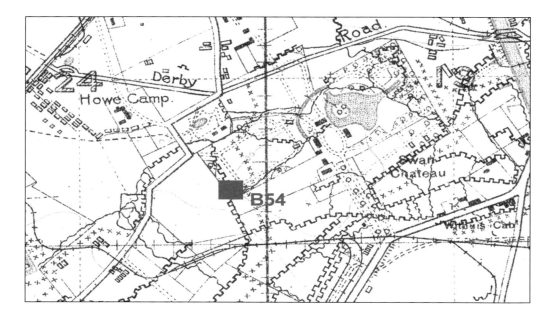

in the winter of 1917/18 when a spring attack by the Germans was being considered likely, it would certainly have been active when the 21st Division held back the Germans in this vicinity during the severe fighting in April 1918, the battles of Kemmel. Through the summer of 1918 this post was within a few hundred yards of the front lines and would have been in constant use. It was a part of what was the Cheapside Line, earlier called GHQ No2 Line, which the Germans were unable to penetrate. It is shown in the photo on the previous page and the map illustrates how it fitted into the trench system.

B55 Hellfire Corner (50.847248, 2.913442).
Just inside the tree line to the west of the Zuiderring N37 about 250 yards south of the modern roundabout which had been the junction known as Hellfire Corner, is the now overgrown rail cutting of the pre-war Ypres-Staden railway line. At the north end of the copse was a bridge where the Ypres-Menin tramway looped away from the main road to cross the rail line with an over-bridge. As both rail lines were used by the British this junction was an important point, with other light railways connecting nearby, known as Hellfire Junction after the adjacent crossroads and was subject to frequent shelling by the Germans.

BELGIUM

In order to maintain the lines rail engineers of a Light Railway Operating Company or Foreways Company were based close by and for protection a shell-proof shelter was constructed. The constructors did not leave any record although it was most likely about 1916. Trench maps of winter 1916/17, when communication trenches may have been flooded, show a long line of raised breastwork, named the Wall of China, connecting this location with the front line. At the other end of the breastwork a burial ground, today named Perth Cemetery (China Wall), had been established.

The shelter, a typical construction of concrete over elephant iron, is built into the lee of the embankment. An opening in the rear door suggests that it led into a further chamber tunnelled into the bank, now collapsed, probably during construction of the road embankment. This is almost certainly the chamber started by 2nd Canadian Tunnelling Company and finished by 177 Tunnelling Company Royal Engineers in June 1917 as '*dugout accommodation for men at a depth of 5 feet'*.

The function of the shelter almost certainly changed after spring 1918, when the German offensive brought their front line to within fifty yards and the shelter was a part of the British front line defences. At that point it would have been occupied by fighting troops rather than rail engineers. Trench maps of summer 1918 show three shelters here so it is likely that two were destroyed during this period.

Adjacent to the shelter in the undergrowth can be seen, on either side of the cutting, solid bulk brick masonry which is probably the remains of the tram bridge over the rail line which was also destroyed during shelling.

B56 Hellfire Corner (50.846364, 2.911168).

Just outside the southern edge of the tree line and clearly visible from the Zuiderring N37, is another bunker of standard British pattern, built on the upper edge of the rail cutting, almost certainly by different troops to the previous entry and dating from 1916 – early 1917. It too is likely to have been associated with the rail system: at this point was a siding from the main Ypres line, known as Gordon House Siding and a depot for supplies and ammunition of which the Germans would have been aware and would have tried to disrupt operations here with shell fire. This bunker may have been built for the safety of the depot troops who could shelter during bombardments. When the German front line came to within a hundred yards of this point in spring 1918 fighting troops would have used this as a front-line shelter.

Two vents in the back wall show that a degree of warmth was provided by fires; the shelter still contains the inner lining of elephant-iron and imprints of sandbags in the outer concrete illustrate the extra cover which was provided externally. These are apparent in the photograph above.

B57 Menin Road South (50.849172, 2.905532).

Just outside the perimeter wall of Menin Road South Cemetery, in the private grounds of the adjoining house, can be seen a masonry-clad concrete bunker. This was most likely a part of the Field Ambulance facility, a shelter for the medical personnel. The additional blast-wall, possibly erected during occupation and close shelling, in front of the door would have made it impassable for stretchers. Obviously built into a pre-existing brick building which has since disappeared, it is now used as a landscaping and general store.

B58 Hill 62 Museum (Sanctuary Wood) Tunnel (50.836144, 2.945232).
In the grounds of the popular and oft visited museum at Sanctuary Wood,
which is on many battlefield tourists' itinerary, are the remains of a trench
complex where Border Lane met Fort Lane and Hill Street trenches. The
trenches have been cleared and re-revetted for maintenance from time to time
but are essentially in their original position. A tunnel or subway, which
comprises reinforced concrete mine frames or panels for wall and roof
supports, connects Fort Lane and Hill Street. The concrete panels also form
the floor, providing rigidity to the section. The panels have nibs cast into
them for jointing. They are continuous, lining the complete four sides, rather
than at regular intervals as may be expected with mine or tunnel timbers in
clay. This is because the ground here on the higher ground is sandy clay and
not fine solid clay as in much of the Ypres salient.

The tunnels are not for offensive mining or for accommodation. With a
very low roof and narrow width, suitable only for single file traffic, they were
for safe communication between fighting trenches.

It is not recorded who constructed the subway, but it was possibly the 2nd
Canadian Tunnelling Company, who were very active here. It may not have
been tunnelled but cut, the panels placed and then covered. Whichever unit
did the work would have required several hundreds of the concrete frames
and it is likely that a factory would have been set up somewhere near Ypres
to manufacture them.

Close to the tunnel entrance is a small dugout consisting of pre-cast concrete blocks, probably dating from a different period.

The photograph above, of the tunnel entrance in Fort Lane, shows the section and panelling.

B59 Cork Cottage (50.852728, 2.915245).

Behind the modern house at the lower end of what was Cavalry Road, nowadays Kruiskalsijdestraat N345, is a concrete shelter which had been built into one of the group of farm buildings which were here known as Cork Cots. A long communication trench, Cork Lane, connected the site to Ypres town.

This is a typical style of British shelter, being an elephant-iron sheet interior with a layer of concrete over for strength and shell protection. It was constructed by an unknown and unrecorded unit, probably as an artillery battery HQ before or during the Third Ypres battles in 1917. Before August it was about ¾ mile from the front line and through the autumn and winter of 1917/18 it was well behind the fighting lines, however after the British withdrawal in April 1918 the location came to be right on the front line. The German line of summer 1918 was less than a hundred yards away but fortunately the structure was not hit by artillery. It is today used as a storeroom by the owner.

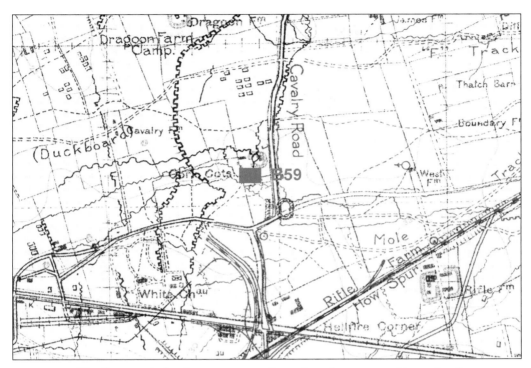

The formwork for the concrete walls and roof, corrugated iron sheeting, can be plainly seen in the photograph below. Until cleared and the garden renovated, the shelter had retained some of the earth covering which had been there since the war. The map is from May 1918, when Cavalry Road was the front line.

235

B60 Hussar Farm (50.858171, 2.914915) Potijze.

At the upper end of Kruiskalssidjestraat (known during the war as Cavalry Road), jutting up above the farm buildings is a tall concrete observation post, which gives views over much of the area to the east where the German lines were. It can be seen that the concrete walls still contain much of the brickwork masonry of the original buildings of the farm, which was known to the British as Hussar Farm. Other farms nearby had similarly derived names, such as Cavalry Farm and Dragoon Farm.

The observation post, which is well constructed, with steel reinforcement, has withstood the effect of a direct artillery hit on the German-facing side which this has caused limited damage. The method of construction, using the original brick walls, corrugated steel and sandbags, can be determined on the exterior. On the interior a ladder of steel rungs leads to the observation platform in what was the roof of the building. The cellar of the farmhouse, directly beneath the upper structure, was also used as a below-

ground shelter, and the remaining wall, cast against sandbags which are evident, of an adjoining bunker can be seen.

The post was probably built in the summer of 1916 by Royal Artillery troops for their own use. Contrary to some reports, it is not Observation Post 11, Red Tiled House, built by the Royal Monmouthshire Royal Engineers. This was 600 yards away to the east and was demolished in the 1970s. A nearby bunker, which formed part of that position, does still exist (see B61). Another, similar observation post, Hasler House at St Jean, had been started by the artillery troops and then taken over and completed by the RMREs.

The pictures left show the post and protected shelter, probably the telephone control to the gun batteries, beneath which the original shape of the farm building and walls can be seen, with the brick walls and roof space. The first picture is shortly post war, with the same view today.

B61Red Tiled House (50.856859, 2.908062) Potijze.
Down a small cul-de-sac, almost opposite the 1km road marker, off Zonnebeekseweg N332, at Potijze is a small concrete shelter which is all that remains of a large observation post, RAOP No.11, which was built into the house opposite (Red Tiled House) and demolished in the 1970s. A modern house stands there now.

The remaining shelter is a fairly weak structure, comprised of some brickwork masonry and very poorly cast concrete in several sections. Although it seems to be associated with the observation post, which was

constructed and recorded in 1916 by the Royal Monmouthshire Royal Engineers, that construction was to a high standard. When a hit by a heavy German shell this caused little damage so the constructors surveyed, photographed and recorded the impact for information for future works. The remaining bunker would be unlikely to withstand an artillery hit. Forming a small chamber with several doorways, it may have been a later addition to the OP by artillery troops.

B62 Vlamertinge Chateau (50.860950, 2.817403).

In the grounds behind Vlamertinge Chateau (which is private land and guarded by a gamekeeper) is an almost perfectly intact Moir Pill Box. It was constructed in the summer of 1918 on what was the Vlamertinghe Line, part of the Green Line defence system, probably by Royal Engineers of 49th Division assisted by American engineers.

By 1918 the chateau had received many hits from German artillery and the place was in ruins. A visiting American engineer, at this stage with little experience of the front, described the chateau which

> 'has been hit many times, but has now been turned into a regular strongpoint or fortified house. It is surrounded by trenches and if the line of trenches is attacked will make an exceedingly strong point...the chateau grounds, once very beautiful, are now criss-crossed with trenches, trees broken and killed, weeds everywhere, and general appearance of neglect and ruin, and that is what you see on every side up here near the front'.[16]

However, others had formed a different opinion. Second Lieutenant Edmund Blunden, passing with the Royal Sussex (1st South Downs) on his way to attack St Julien in 1917 and seeing the chateau and the artillery battery, wrote:

> *'This must be the floweriest place*
> *That earth allows; the queenly face*
> *Of the proud mansion borrows grace for grace*
> *Spite of those brute guns lowing at the skies.'*
>   Vlamertinghe (Passing the Chateau, July 1917)

The Moir Pill Box and the other defences were not used as the Germans did not come within range and survived the post-war clearing up. It still contains the protective revolving steel ring and gun carriage and traces of camouflage.

B63 Vlamertinghe Chateau (50.861417, 2.815676).

Also in the chateau grounds, about 200 yards to the north-west of the Moir in a wooded area, is a large concrete bunker, nowadays overgrown and difficult to enter, which was most probably the command post for the 9.2-inch gun battery, probably 154 Siege Battery, located on the western edge of the wood in the summer of 1918 and firing throughout the summer. The various batteries here earlier would have been active for most stages of the fighting east of Ypres.

Below are the artillery command bunker and the Moir Pill Box in the chateau grounds.

B64 (50.868852, 2.837412), B65 (50.866580, 2.839258), B66 (50.866398, 2.838796) Brielen (Trois Tours Chateau).

In the north-eastern corner of the grounds of the chateau known as Trois Tours, nowadays Kastell Drie Torens, is a concrete machine gun pill box overlooking the flat land to the east, with gun embrasure having a wide field of fire. This is one of the earliest such constructions, on either side, during the Great War. On 14 August 1915 the 456th (1/2nd West Riding) Field Company Royal Engineers, 49th Division, recorded starting a *'concrete MG emplacement'* here, mixing and placing 35 cwt (about 1.8 tonnes) of concrete each day; on 28 August work was held up because of lack of cement by which stage they were fitting the roof and the construction was *'slowly progressing'*.

Although well behind the front line, the defences around the chateau were being bolstered as the Germans were still trying to press westwards, and the division was aware of a potential assault by them.

The chateau, which had been completely renovated in 1892, was used as an HQ by many divisions throughout the war (the 1st Canadian Division during the 1915 Battle of Ypres, and later the 38th Welsh Division had its HQ here for the opening of the 3rd Ypres battle) and fortunately suffered little damage. It was used as a registration office by the (then) Imperial War Graves Commission after the war, and is today much as it was then.

The pill box is overgrown with ivy and herbage so it is difficult to examine the exterior. It shows signs of method of formwork and construction, with sand-bag formwork evident and the incorporation of masonry bricks at the

rear. Built onto the east-facing elevation of the roof is an infantry protection parapet, about twenty inches high, designed for rifle or machine gun fire from the roof. The inside is large enough to accommodate a number of infantrymen as well as a machine gun crew. This is an unusual design for a British construction,

although similar designs with the ability to fire from within or from the top were later used by the Germans.

Also in the grounds are two other concrete shelters, B65 and B66. Whilst not identical externally, these are both of similar design to one another, with almost identical floor plans and interior, built probably by the same engineers. It is likely that they are shelters for the staff in the chateau, for use in case of prolonged artillery bombardments or aerial attack; due to the house being built on a small island with surrounding moat, there are no cellars which normally would have been used for this. Such shelter became necessary as in 1917 and 1918 siege batteries, such as 5th Siege Battery and 309th Honourable Artillery Company ('London Gunners') were based around the wood and, being involved in counter-battery work, attracted in-coming heavy artillery fire in reply.

B67 Brielen (50.867814, 2.847232).
This village was well defended throughout the period between 1915 and spring 1918, but from then on, with the expectation of a German offensive and planned British withdrawal from the land captured in 1917, defences were greatly increased and the village was arranged as an area of resistance or strongpoint, designed to prevent enemy progress. The village was surrounded by trenches and barbed wire with many machine gun positions. The surviving concrete shelter in the village, which is situated in the back garden of a house opposite the church on the other side of the N8 Ypres-Veurne road (Vuernesweg), was probably a command post for defence of the village, and utilised as a shelter by one of the artillery batteries meanwhile. It is a long and thin construction, comprising a concrete shell roof over elephant iron, with brickwork end walls. There are two entrances, one in an end wall and one through the west-facing wall.

BELGIUM

B68 Wagram Farm (50.876462, 2.850190).

Just inside the wooded area behind the farm on the west side of Reningsestraat which had been known as Wagram Farm, is a double-chambered shelter, with a corridor at each end and protected entrance hallway at the rear with steps down. The name Wagram was given to the nearby farm by the French when they held this sector in 1915. As with other farms nearby, such as Solferino, Malakoff, Leipzig, Friedland and Jena Farms, it was named after a French Napoleonic battle success. Napoleon defeated the Austrians at

the Battle of Wagram near Vienna in 1809.

The shelter, partly sunken and with earth covering, was probably a command post for infantry in the reserve line or an artillery battery behind the wood. A light railway ran adjacent to the wood, past the shelter and on towards the canal and the front line about 1½ miles to the east. In spring

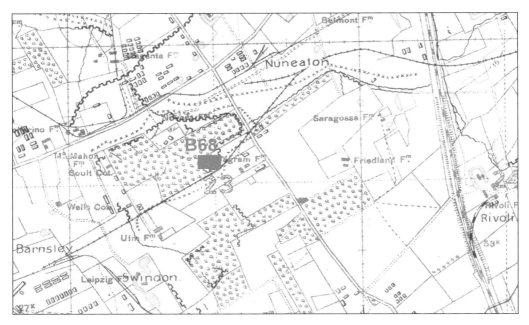

243

1918 the area was strengthened for defence, the wood surrounded by trenches and this shelter would have been incorporated into the defences.

The two figures on the previous page show the entrance and location of the shelter.

B68A Elverdinge (50.881867, 2.825562)

In the grounds of a private house on Veurnsweg, the N8 towards Ypres (this road did not exist during the war, the original Ypres road is now the parallel Sint Livinusstraat) south of the village, in the plot south of Hotel Nicolas, is a large partly subterranean double-chambered bunker. Probably part of what was Field Camp, or for one of the many artillery batteries sited around here, it is of similar design to the one at Wagram Farm and is possibly the work of the same constructors. The outer walls show the typical sandbag formwork texture with elephant-iron inner forms. The bunker is unused today as it is often flooded and is partly hidden by a screen of ornamental trees; but in 1988 the householder built onto it a summer house.

BELGIUM

B69 Boezinge Chateau (50.894649, 2.856606).

In the wooded grounds of Boezinge Chateau, which is private property, is one of the larger British constructions still existing on the Western Front. It is a solid double-chambered shelter, built into what was an outhouse of the chateau in preparation for the planning of the attack on the German lines on the other side of the canal. The sector was held by the Guards Division, who held the northernmost part of the British line for the 1917 offensive to push the Germans away from the salient and eastwards in what became the Third Battle of Ypres.

Several battalions of the Guards had headquarters in the chateau, which was much damaged after three years of artillery bombardment by the Germans (the front line was only 500 yards away) and it was decided to construct shell-proof accommodation for planning and controlling the forthcoming battle. Royal Engineers attached to the Guards – 75th and 76th Field Companies – constructed the shelter, incorporating much of the original brickwork for camouflage and formwork, and made it functional for the infantrymen, white-washing the interior to increase light. The 1st Battalion Coldstream Guards established their HQ here, and then the 2nd and 4th Scots Guards and the 4th Grenadier Guards.

The Guards were already aware of the advantages of concrete shell-proof cover as they had been raiding the German lines opposite for some time and had experience of their suitability. On one such raid Lieutenant Mahomed and No.10 Platoon of 1st Scots Guards crossed the canal on canvas mats during the night of 25/26 June and examined the German shelters, which he termed 'concrete dug-outs', that they were to attack a few days later. Lieutenant Mahomed reported on the German defences but was killed during the main attack on 31st July.

Prior to and following the attack many wounded were treated here and a number were buried in a cemetery which was established in the chateau grounds. The burials were later re-interred at Artillery Wood Cemetery on the other side of the canal.

The photos on the following page show how the shelter appeared during the war, during a quiet period, probably later in 1917, and as it is today amongst the trees which have since grown.

B70 Boezinge (50.893776, 2.859149).
On the main street through Boezinge, Diksmuidweg, behind the demarcation stone which marks the extent of the German advance in 1914 before they were repulsed back across the canal, is an ivy-covered concrete and brick observation post. Constructed to give a field of view along what is nowadays Brugstratt, towards the canal and over into what were the German lines beyond, it was probably used by observation officers of the artillery, who could observe the accuracy of fire from here.

B71 Boezinge (Canal Bank 1) (50.891756, 2.868311).
In the canal embankment to the southeast of Boezinge, about 100 yards down the Westkaaipad (canal-side footpath) past the lock which did not exist during the war, is a concrete shelter which was built on the British front line in 1917. The German front line – named Canal Trench by the British – was directly opposite on the other side of the canal and both sides would have been watching each other across the water and mud which comprised the canal. The proximity can be discerned from the photo below.

Built at embankment level, it would have been manned by an observer using a periscope to maintain a watch for any movements. It is situated at what was the boundary of the Guards and 38th (Welsh) Divisions at the opening of the attack on 31 July 1917, at the junction of where the canal-side trench, known as section B12.1, met with the trench numbered S1 which ran here from the railway station.

247

B71A Boezinge (Canal Bank 2) 50.877105, 2.870151.
Tunnelled into the mound which was the spoil from the canal cutting south of Boezinge on the Diksmuidsweg, directly opposite Bard Cottage Cemetery, can be seen the front and top edges of a concrete shelter. The embankment has since been levelled and straightened which has partly covered and hidden it. Royal Engineers of 208th (Norfolk) Field Company, 34th Division had their headquarters here in October 1917 when infantrymen of the division were attempting to cross the Broenbeek near Langemarck (today there is a memorial to the 34th Division there).

During this period the engineers were involved in maintaining the foot and light rail bridges over the canal and the trackways over the battlefield towards the front lines which the Germans kept shelling to interrupt the transport of men and materials to the fighting zone. This was very dangerous work and the engineers lost men during this period, some of whom, including Lieutenant Bennett, are buried in Bard Cottage Cemetery, on the opposite side of the road.

B72 Essex Farm Orderly Room (50.873173, 2.871910).
Further south along the canal bank, to the north of Essex Farm ADS, can be seen an earth mound and low concrete wall which are the remains of the Royal Engineers Orderly Room. It was constructed by engineers of 38th Division as their HQ whilst the division held the line and they provided engineering support to the troops in the fighting zone and maintained the bridges across the canal which were the lifeline of the infantry operations. The Germans were aware of these bridges and kept up frequent shelling to destroy them.

Whilst based in this Orderly Room, discipline for the sappers was maintained; on 7 May 1917 a trial was held in this bunker for an unspecified offence. The diary of 124th Field Company records:

'92575 Sapper DM Grace of this Company tried by Field General Court Martial at Company HQ. Sentenced to 90 days F.P. No.1.'

The engineers were obviously proud of their office and placed a plaque, which is still evident, stating that it is the Orderly Room, over the doorway. This is shown inset although rather damaged by the concrete cracking from the stress of the movement and settling of the earthworks.

B73 Essex Farm North (50.872969, 2.872163).
A hundred yards to the north of Essex Farm ADS is the remnant of a dugout which had been constructed – probably by 124th Field Company in March 1917 – for the shelter and protection of troops who were supporting the front line infantry on the other (eastern) side of the canal. For much of the time this shelter housed Royal Engineers, particularly those of the 38th (Welsh) Division whose office was adjacent.

It shows the typical construction method of elephant-iron sheeting (largely corroded away) with concrete end walls, and a doorway and windows facing away from the front. In this instance the elephant-iron has been placed on concrete side walls to give height internally. There is also evidence of a masonry brick and concrete shelter which had adjoined it. This construction was earth covered and sandbagged to improve protection. Despite much shelling in the vicinity, it survived undamaged and was used in the immediate post-war years as accommodation by a local family.

The later collapse of all the earthworks, and probable post-war removal and re-use elsewhere of bricks, resulted in the bunker being partly earth filled and hidden except for the top half of the front wall. Later excavated and cleaned up by local archaeologists, it can now be visited and is a good example of both method of construction and siting behind the high ground of the canal bank.

BELGIUM

B74 Essex Farm ADS (50.871731, 2.873048).
The series of shelters which were Essex Farm Dressing Station is one of the more frequently visited sites in the Ypres area and in recent years have been tidied up and made accessible to visiting parties, with paved footpaths and improved drainage. Concrete parapet retaining walls on top of the shelters, which were about three feet high and held back the earth covering, were removed during this refurbishment. For many years the shelters stood empty and abandoned except for a few interested visitors and tourists. Nowadays it is on almost all itineraries, sometimes with bus-loads of sightseers to this and the adjacent cemetery and John McCrae site.

The existing concrete bunkers are the result of several years of constant up-grading and improving of the accommodation. The canal bank had been a continuous line of shelters and dugouts tunnelled into it, both to the south, towards Ypres where the bank height reduced, and to the north, where it maintained sufficient cover for some quite large bunkers. Other Dressing Stations – Sussex Farm, Fusilier Farm and St John's – had also been constructed into the bank but do not exist today. Medical and organisational centres had been in operation here since the middle of 1915, when the front to the east of the canal settled after the Canadians and British divisions established themselves here.

The 6th Division spent the latter part of 1915 and spring of 1916 here, and organised their medical facilities. Even though the area was a relatively 'quiet' zone, with no major offensive but many small scale operations, the division reported almost 11,000 casualties whilst holding this sector of the Salient. The 20th (Light) Division also recorded heavy losses whilst holding the line here. Many of the wounded would have been treated at Essex Farm, mainly at that time comprising simple shrapnel-proof accommodation which had been produced by 509th Field Company RE. The 2/2nd London Field Ambulance were based here and kept busy for a period.

The 38th (Welsh) Divisional engineers spent some time late in 1916 improving the accommodation and in the middle of December it was handed over to 134th Field Ambulance RAMC as the Essex Farm Advanced Dressing Station. The chambers included an operating theatre and several wards and treatment rooms. At some time the shelters were decorated internally to make them more welcoming and comfortable, with a line of fleurs-de-lys painted on at dado height in the end chamber, with some blue paint still plainly visible. Other chambers were whitewashed and some of these contain graffiti, such as from personnel of 133 Field Ambulance, although some is more modern.

With the planning for the 1917 offensive the ADS was handed over to the 1/3rd Highland Field Ambulance. They recorded it as

'Numerous dug-outs for accommodation of patients and stores. Shell proof building for two motor ambulances' and 'a very well built and well protected Advanced Dressing Station with electric light. There are numerous dug-outs for accommodation and a shell-proof building for the two motor ambulances kept there.'

The Germans were aware of much activity in the area of the ADS and frequently shelled it. The Assistant Director of Medical Services for the 51st (Highland) Division recorded several instances of shelling with direct hits causing damage, and decided on 11 July to reduce the manning levels. It stayed in use throughout the battles of 1917, after burials were stopped in the cemetery adjoining, and continued in use into September 1918 in several military functions, after which the whole front moved away to the east with the German withdrawal from the Salient.

A close examination of the concrete shelter shows that it is very well constructed, although a lack of reinforcing steel is apparent in some parts. The shifting forward of the front walls and major cracking – including the up-lifting of the floor – is the result of pressure from the earth bank behind,

as was the partial collapse of the roof parapet retaining walls, and is not apparent in post-war photographs. The pictures left show the ADS whilst in use during a quiet period of the war, and above during the 1930s when it was abandoned and overgrown; it was in a similar condition up to the 1980s. Today it is easily accessible and much photographed.

B75 Lancashire Farm (50.881214, 2.883385).

The underground concrete shelter in the field off Kleine Poezelstraat, which is a single chamber of thick concrete roof with an elephant-iron lining, was built into the farm that stood here in the early years of the war, being only a few hundred yards behind the front line (the existing farm is about a hundred yards north of the original). Although it was named Lancashire Farm, the trenches in the immediate area all carried Yorkshire names, such as Mirfield Trench which lay directly alongside, with Headingly, Huddersfield and Skipton Trenches nearby. The road named Kleine Poezelstraat was named Huddleston Road by the British. Captain P.G. Huddleston, Commanding Officer of 84th Field Company Royal Engineers, was killed nearby whilst inspecting no man's land on 25 March 1916. He was buried the day after in Ferme-Olivier Cemetery.

The farm was occupied by several units of the 49th (West Riding), 38th (Welsh) Divisions and others (Guards, 6th, 14th, 20th and 39th Divisions) as through 1915, 1916 and 1917 it became an important location as headquarters for the battalions holding the line here. Several improvements and modifications were made to the facilities and the defences were strengthened by various field and tunnelling companies of engineers. Early in 1917 tunnels were dug beneath the farm and in 1998 archaeological investigations discovered a deep vertical shaft, 40 feet deep, 6 feet in diameter, lined with steel tubing, which connected with corridor tunnels which ran for some distance but had collapsed. A later investigation revealed a number of tunnel entrances which have since been covered and closed.

It was probably whilst the Royal Welsh Fusiliers and Welsh Regiment were based here in May 1916 that the 1st (Siege) Company Royal Monmouthshire Royal Engineers constructed a concrete tower for an artillery OP, but this does not exist today. Whilst the 39th Division were here in February 1917 the 227 Field Company carried out improvements and later, in April, the 123 and 124 Field Companies of the 38th (Welsh) Division continued strengthening the position and the HQ of the Welsh battalions and this is probably the shelter which exists today. In August 1915 a light railway, Lancashire Farm Tramline, which crossed the canal near Bard's Cottage Cemetery, had been laid to terminate at the farm ruins, which eased the supply

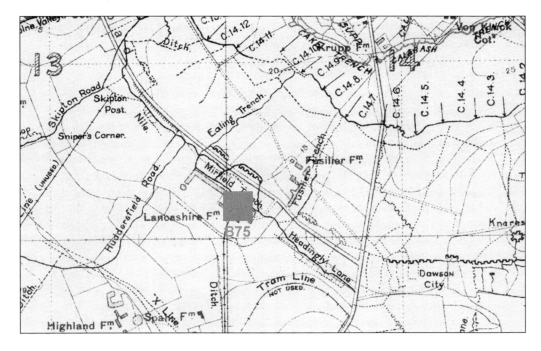

of engineering materials, and a telephone line was laid with connection to other units and the Divisional HQ at Trois Tours Chateau.

The shelter was passed by waves of Welshmen of 114 Brigade who went in to the attack the German front lines and beyond on 31 July 1917, though until September 1918 it was surrounded by army hutting, with another light railway line laid to the shelter. It was excavated and examined in 2004 before being largely re-covered.

The photo above shows the bunker shortly after excavation, with the original trench boards at the threshold, and the location on a 1917 trench map.

B76 (50.861925, 2.901716) St Jan.

Behind a farm on the southern side of the Brugseweg, N323 the Ypres-Potijze road, almost level with White House cemetery, in the angle formed by the Bellewaardebeek, is a solidly built and strong angular shelter showing obvious signs of being formed against corrugated iron sheets. Internally it has a single chamber formed over elephant iron, with a ventilation hole probably for a stove. It does not have an embrasure, nor any obvious facility for placing a machine gun over the roof; it appears to be a shell-proof accommodation shelter with no record of its construction. There is no agricultural or civilian building marked on contemporary maps, so it was not cast inside an existing building, although maps of late 1917/early 1918 show some hutted accommodation here. It was probably cast for one of the artillery field battery positions following the British withdrawal in April 1918, to place it about a mile from the front lines.

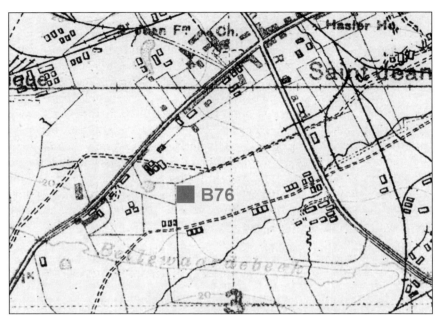

At some stage it seems to have received a hit by a German shell although this has only caused minor damage. It may have been after this that an additional wall was cast to provide extra protection to the entrance.

BELGIUM

B77 (50.855505, 2.989129), B77A (50.855213, 2.989429) Polygon Wood.
In the north east of Polygon Wood, or Polygoneveld, about 150 yards west
of Buttes New British Cemetery, are two small simple shelters built in the
typical style of several feet of concrete over an elephant-iron sheet lining.

After the 5th Australian Division pushed the Germans eastwards and out
of Polygon Wood, several other British and the New Zealand Divisions held
the sector whilst continuing to press forward until the fighting was scaled
down in November. The New Zealanders, part of II Anzac Corps, occupied
the wood in December 1917 and into January 1918, during which a strong
defence scheme was put into place, including an outpost line, front and
support line systems and second or corps line to the rear. The top end of
Polygon Wood was in the support line, with wire belts and trenches running
through the wood and more accommodation, in addition to the existing
German shelters in the wood, was needed.

By now the trees had been reduced to a few stumps, with occasional
upright bare trunks, after severe shelling by both sides. The position was
under the observation of German artillery spotters at Polderhoek Chateau,

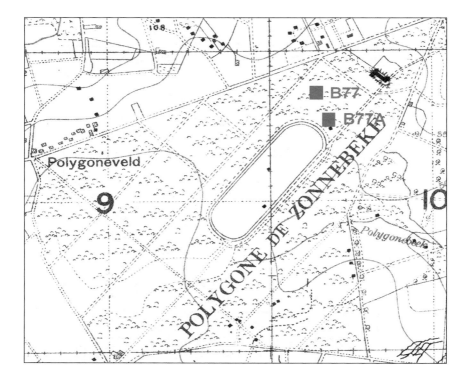

257

across the Reutelbeek, and during this period of occupation when neither side was attacking, conditions can be imagined from the number of NZ troops who died and are commemorated on the New Zealand Memorial at the Buttes.

The 4th Field Company New Zealand Engineers constructed two concrete shelters, which they recorded as being suitable to accommodate four men each, these are marked on later Anzac maps as Battalion HQ.

For many years the two shelters were overgrown and hidden by undergrowth and bracken, however in recent years they have been made more accessible and a pathway to them cut through the wood. They can be found in a section of the wood named Plantagiebos 10, just to the right of the track which runs south into the wood from Buttes New British Cemetery. They are shown in the photographs below and marked on the map (the racetrack, which was the driving track of the Belgian artillery school in the wood before the war, is not evident today).

B78 View Farm (50.874482, 2.902523).
In the small field adjacent to the shrine to Our Lady of Peace on what was known as Buffs Road (named after the 1st Battalion, the Buffs, East Kent Regiment who held the line in early June 1915), nowadays Hogeziekenweg, is the visible roof of a larger underground construction which was probably related to the large hutment collection, Hill Top Camp. The camp was located here later in 1917 after the front had moved eastwards and was enlarged in 1918. This had been an important location throughout the 'quiet' years of late 1915 and 1916. Being almost on the crest of a contour which gave views over the German lines, the farm had therefore early on in the war been named View Farm, and less than a hundred yards to the north was Hill Top Farm, which sat atop the crest. Much activity had taken place here, including the provision in summer 1916 of an observation post for the Royal Artillery in one of the few trees which grew here.

When the British planned to withdraw from the areas in the east for which they had fought so hard, defences on high ground such as this at View Farm – which needed to be denied to the Germans because of the views it afforded over Ypres – were bolstered. Many trenches and defence strong points were dug and this construction probably dates from that period.

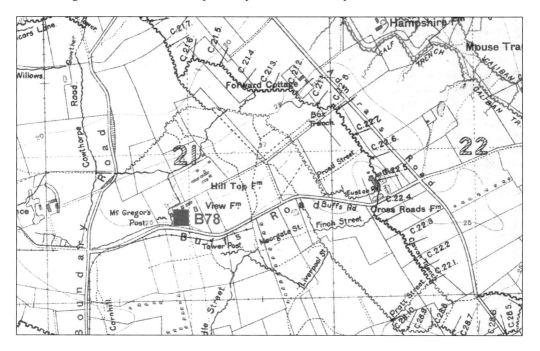

The roof of the shelter is shown above, and the map shows the view from the location, over the British front line, no man's land and the German front line at Caliban Trench, upper right.

B79 Tuff's Farm (50.909619, 2.902000).
Between Pilckem and Pilckem Langemarck, about a hundred yards south of Ruisseau Farm Cemetery, on a sharp bend on Melkerijstraat (Dairy Street) and adjacent to modern farm buildings, is a two-part concrete construction – a British shelter tacked on to a German machine gun pill box. The pill box, one of several in the locality, was in what was left of the buildings of Tuff's Farm, which held up the Guards Division advance on the opening day of the Ypres offensive, known as the Battle of Pilckem. It was finally taken and the gun silenced by troops of 2nd Grenadier Guards, who passed forward to the Steenbeck, a hundred yards further down Melkerijstraat, where they dug in under heavy German fire from the other side of the stream and from Langemarck.

The bridge over the Steenbeck – nowadays where the road into the Milcobel dairyfoods factory is closed – was named Tuff's Bridge. It is not known who Tuff was or why the name was given to the farm and bridge, but the name first appears on maps in early July 1917 just before the battle commenced. Once dug in, the Grenadiers were relieved by the 1st Irish Guards. For several weeks this pill box was close to the front line and would have been an important shelter for the British during the ensuing battle of Langemarck, being occupied by units of the 37th and 18th Divisions.

In January 1918 it was decided to utilise the German construction over

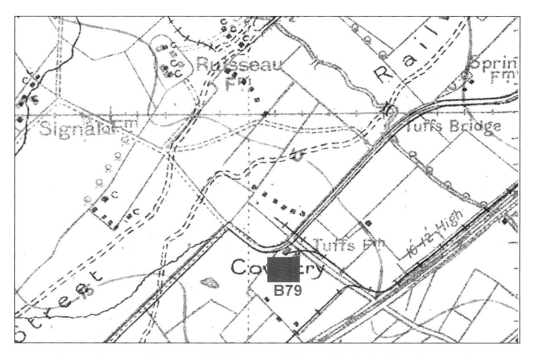

the coming months as the British were still hopeful of a further advance. To simplify entry from the western side it was necessary to cut a new doorway. The 135th Army Troops Company RE were given the task and allocated three sections to the work. They found cutting through the concrete extremely hard and recorded:

> 'difficulty was experienced in keeping sections supplied with tools for pill box work, the concrete being very hard and breaking points of tools. Used gun cotton to break up the concrete.'

Later a new adjacent concrete shelter was added to the pill box, behind the original German one, in anticipation of a possible German offensive. The 256th Tunnelling Company RE constructed this (as a 'repair and addition') in the first days of April 1918, with a labour force of eleven engineers and forty-nine attached infantry.

About the same time a spur of a light railway off the nearby main line, which had recently been re-laid with light rail by the engineers, was laid to Tuff's Farm where it terminated and was named 'Coventry' and was a supply point.

This dual German/British bunker is today the sole remnant of many such which were in this area. The picture below shows the small British addition, cast against corrugated iron and largely buried in farm materials, butting up to the larger original German emplacement which is nowadays used to house ducks. The map shows the location, just south of Ruisseau Farm Cemetery.

B80 Wimbledon (50.890296, 2.977936).

At Graventafelstraat, about a hundred yards south-west of the New Zealand memorial, is a small British bunker which probably dates from February 1918, when the engineers of 1st (Home Counties) Field Company, 8th Division, were constructing shelters for headquarters of infantry battalions holding the Gravenstafel defence line after the crossroads and higher land to the east had been captured by the New Zealanders on 4 October. The New Zealand engineers had surveyed the area for troop accommodation; there were a number of German pill boxes in the vicinity – including three directly opposite on the other side of the road – but these have not survived.

The 8th Division recorded the appalling winter conditions which troops endured during this period, with plank roads being washed away and *'men*

sank deep into ice-cold clinging mud and had to be dug out'. The location is marked 'Wimbledon' on contemporary trench maps. It is sheltered in the lee of this rising ground. Cast against corrugated iron internally, and with the exterior sandbags clearly apparent, these, with the possible addition of burster blocks on top, would have helped to provide extra protection in the event of an artillery hit.

B81 Ypres Railway Station (50.849205, 2.874432)
In the waste land behind Ypres railway station, adjacent to the disused canal, is the remnant of what had been a larger concrete shelter, with a strong reinforced concrete roof laid on steel rails. Maps between 1915 and 1918 show this point to be the terminus of light gauge rail lines laid by the British running to the south of the salient. It is likely that this structure was to provide protection to engines or rail personnel as the Germans shelled the area regularly throughout the war.

B82 (50.895038, 2.773919), B83 (50.893685, 2.773758) Wippe.
The hamlet of Wippe, on the road between Poperinge and Woesten, was a very busy supply area for much of the war, especially the build-up to the 1917 offensive. In the land immediately north of the road junction De Wippe Cabaret (named Gilford Cross Roads on trench maps) was one of the main rail sidings, Ondank, for storage and supplies of engineering materials. The area around the cross roads had many hutments, with Box Camp occupying the present houses.

At some stage, probably early in 1918, two double-roomed concrete shelters were constructed, probably for protection from artillery bombardment. The shelters and much of the hutting was out of direct sight of the German infantry, being just behind the low crest of the twenty metre contour, but the importance of the area was known to them who gave it much artillery attention. It is likely that Belgian Army engineers had a rôle in the construction of the shelters, as the sector was to be handed over to them as the British were preparing to pull back from the land gained in 1917 and the Belgians were to take over the northern area and facilities. The Commander of II Corps, which had held the northern sector of the Ypres salient and the Pilckem Ridge through the winter of 1917 and into spring 1918, reported in early June that:

'last winter No.256 Tunnelling Company was employed by the II Corps on the construction of concrete pill-boxes with very great success. These shelters are now being used by the Belgian Army and have withstood very well the enemy's artillery fire'.

Some of the shelters referred to existed until around 2005, such as at Colonel's Farm and Major's Farm, both on Pilckem Ridge, when they were demolished.

For both constructions at Wippe – which are well constructed with strong walls and roofs – use was made of the existing farm buildings for cover and screening. Both have small windows adjacent to the double doors and internal whitewashing shows signs of increasing illumination. Additionally, both still have some of the original wood formwork panelling on the inside. The shelters were used by the Belgian Army during the summer of 1918 until they took part in the offensive in September to push the Germans eastwards.

B84 (51.112488, 2.740391) Ramskapelle (Steenbakkerij).
The tall tower, the chimney of the pre-war brickworks on Koolhofstraat, is clearly visible for some distance around. It gave commanding views over the area beyond Nieuwpoort and Ramskapelle and the land to the east occupied by the Germans. The original brick chimney had been concreted with access ladders, which are still visible, leading to a platform on the top. It can be seen that a direct hit on the top of the chimney has caused cracking part way down, although the tower did not topple. It is possibly one of the artillery

observation towers constructed and recorded by 148th Army Troops Company in October 1917; Royal Engineers of the 42nd Division also record working whilst based here in 1917, when the division held the coastal sector, later to be relieved by the French army.

B85 (51.072060, 2.792169) Pervijze.
On entering the village from Diksmuide can be seen the tall observation post which gave good views over the flat land to the east and the wet areas between the Belgian and German lines. One of the main tasks of the observers in the post was to watch for the firing of Lange Max, a 380mm German gun at Leugenboom, four miles away; this had been constructed to bombard Dunkirk and began firing in June 1917. With a barrel of 17.5 metres it was at that time the longest and biggest gun in the world. The observers, on seeing the gun fire, immediately signalled the event and a loud steam whistle was sounded in the town to alert the inhabitants. The shells, which weighed 750kg, took ninety seconds to reach their target.

The post, built of pre-cast concrete blocks inside what had been the walls of the presbytery of St Catherine's church (which was not rebuilt after the war), is today leaning as a result of partial subsidence (the tower has separated from the side wall); the constructors were more concerned with durability from shell damage than from long term level. It has obviously withstood many artillery hits.

The 148th Army Troops Company RE recorded in October 1917 that they were busy constructing artillery observation posts in old buildings in Pervijze and Ramskappelle and it is probably this unit which made the existing post. As they were doing much concrete work in the area they managed to obtain a petrol driven concrete mixer – not a luxury possessed by many engineer units.

The photos show the post after construction in the remains of the house, and in recent times. The brickwork on top of the tower dates from German usage during World War Two.

There are many other concrete constructions in the area between Boezinge and the coast at Nieuwpoort; some date from when the French held the sector and some from the brief period when the British held the coastal area. When the Belgians held this part of their own land between 1915 and 1918 they

were busy actively bolstering defences with shell-proof shelters and machine gun emplacements, a number of these constructions still exist. Royal Engineers of many companies gave assistance with materials supply and construction (the engineers maintained and used the engineering supply dump at Ondank, Wippe, which was in Belgian Army territory), although such work was generally unrecorded in any detail of works carried out or locations given. One exception was 148th Army Troops Company RE who detailed in October 1917 the construction in the gable of the wall at Allaertshuis Farm, near Ramskapelle, of a
concrete observation post camouflaged with brickwork. This was demolished probably during rebuilding of the farmhouse in 1924.

References

1. *Manual of Field Engineering*. General Staff, War Office. 1911/1914.
2. *History of The Corps of Royal Engineers*. Vol V, the First World War. p. 453.
3. *Narrative of the 502 (Wessex) Field Company Royal Engineers 1915-1919*. Major C.L. Fox. 1920, Hugh Rees Ltd.
4. *Official History of the War*, 1917 Vol. 2, p45.
5. *The Official History of Australia in the War of 1914-1918 Vol. IV,* 1917. C.E.W. Bean. p623.
6. *Work of RE in the European War.* Vol. Miscellaneous. p240.
7. War Diary, 6th (Siege) Company, Royal Monmouthshire Royal Engineers.
8. *Work of RE in the European War.* Vol. Miscellaneous. p158.
9. *History of the East Lancashire Royal Engineers.* 1921.
10. *History of the 520th (Field) Company RE (TF) 1914-1918.* War Narratives Publishing Co, London, 1919.
11. War Diary, General Officer Commanding Canadian Machine Gun Corps. Machine Gun Reconnaissance Officer, Appendices, May/June 1918.
12. *History of the 40th Division.* F.W. Whitton. Gale and Polden, 1926.
13. War Diary, Matron-in Charge, British Expeditionary Force (Miss Maud McCarthy) National Archives WO 95/3988-3911.
14. *History of 107th Infantry USA.* Gerald F. Jacobson. New York 1920.
15. *Official History of 120th Infantry (3rd North Carolina).* John Otey Walker. J.P. Bell.
16. Diary of Colonel Joseph Hyde Pratt. Edwards and Broughton, Raleigh. USA

APPENDIX 1

Report on Shoeburyness comparative trials

Q.M.G   DES/752/9168

CONCRETE SHELTERS

On the 21st August I proceeded with Major General Atkinson (C.E. First Army) and Colonel Brady (F.W. 5) to Shoeburyness to watch trials on two concrete shelters there.

The trials were designed to test the vulnerability of these shelters and to test the relative merits of the 2 types of construction in France.

Without giving detailed results of the trials, which are of a very technical nature and will be supplied in due course, accompanied by photos, the following points appeared to be established conclusively.

(a) The Artillery Officers expressed great admiration for the strength of the shelters; in fact they were rather inclined to regard them as an unusual opportunity for testing types of shell. We were able, however, to keep the trials to a form which produced the tests we required and still leave the structures in fair condition for further R.A. trials.

(b) The shelters are absolutely proof against 4.5″ shell at ranges down to 3,000 yards.

(c) The shelters are not upset, nor seriously affected by 8″ shell bursting 12" from the wall of the shelter.

(d) The shelters are not proof against 6′ shell at 3,000 yards; a blind shell penetrates the wall, while a shell which bursts produces a 3′ x 2′ breech. But the structure as a whole remains quite repairable.

(e) The Arques shelter is stronger structurally than the Aire shelter, but owing to the lack of reinforcement in the blocks tends to break in transit. Also for the same reason there is a tendency for the inner $4^{1}/_{2}$″ beyond the reinforcing mesh to flake off under concussion. Some form of reinforcement is necessary. The Aire pattern should preferably have horizontal reinforcing bars.

It is observed that the construction of these shelters means the provision of about 20,000 tons monthly of which 5,000 tons is cement.

Shelter against 4.2" shells can, it is understood, be obtained by the use of large shelters covered with 2 feet of concrete and 3 to 4 feet of earth.

The objection to the manufacture in situ might be met by the provision of concrete voissoir blocks.

It is further noted the use of the concrete shelters as a Machine Gun Pill Box involves the use of 90 tons of material per pill box against the 5 tons per Moir Pill Box.

In view of the changing situation and the cost involved it is submitted that the question of the numbers of these shelters to be provided, and of erection at the present juncture, whilst lines are very flexible, should be considered by the General Staff having in view the result of the trials now made.

26.8.18. (Sgd) J.W.S. Sewell
Brig. General
DIRECTOR OF ENGINEERING STORES

APPENDIX 2

The Moir Pill Box in Britain

A number were incorporated into Britain's coastal defences in 1918. Some, which had then been abandoned, may have been re-incorporated in 1940 when defences were being installed. However they are unlikely to have been used in their intended manner as the special Vickers gun mountings, if still present, would have been removed for scrap or rusted and no records of re-manufacture have been found. As none exist today it is presumed that any remaining were removed during post-World War Two coastal defence clearances.

At the end of World War One some 730 complete Moir Pill Box kits, which had been awaiting transport to France and Belgium, were still sitting at Richborough yard, surplus to requirements. Probably the metal parts were reclaimed, but the many concrete blocks were put to other uses. Due to their shape they were of no use for road making or building; those which did not go for landfill or rubble did find use as earth retaining walls and many of these are still in use today. In Sandwich (St George's Road) and Woodnesborough village can be found several examples, as shown below.

Just outside Sandwich, in a copse by the A256/A257 road junction, and nowadays abandoned and overgrown, is a small compound or stock yard comprising crinkle-crankle walls built using Moir concrete blocks. It has been claimed that this is a defence post dating from the 1940s, however the unmortared, loose-laid blocks and the open aspect makes this unlikely. It was probably a stock or equipment yard used by a farmer or contractor.

APPENDIX 3

Comments on the Moir Pill Box

The Australians did not like the Moir Pill Box and the Chief Engineer of the Australian Corps recorded his comments on viewing the first one erected in their area, with the Chief Engineer of the Fourth Army, on 8 July 1918:

> *'The pill box is not entirely satisfactory. It is composed of interlocking segmental bricks made of reinforced concrete covered by an iron cupola. It is not proof against any common shell, and would be seriously damaged by a direct hit from a 4.2 shell. It can, of course, be vastly improved by putting a wall of concrete either reinforced or not about 3′6″ thick around it, but in this event the segmental bricks would only act as centering and if this is all they are required for they might be much lighter or even dispensed with altogether. The Moir Pill Box will probably be found useful as an O.P. in quiet parts of the line.'*
>
> War Diary, CE Australian Corps, 8th August 1918)

Other comments by Australian Engineer Companies were in a similar vein.

The Australians designed their own factory made pill box, the Hobbs MG Casemate, which was an armour-plated steel cupola with Vickers MG fitting, although this came into production too late to be of any practical use. Field trials began – unsuccessfully – in France in August 1918, as recorded by the Australian Chief Engineer on 20 August:

> *'The Chief Engineer together with the Stores Officer went to Le Touquet to see tests of the HOBBS Cupola at the GHQ Lewis Gun School at that place. A good deal of stress had been laid by General Staff of the Army upon these tests, even to the extent of making a special request for the presence of the Stores Officer, Australian Corps. On arrival at Le Touquet however, it was discovered that the Instructional staff of the School knew very little about the Hobbs*

Cupola and indeed it was not possible to obtain the Vickers Machine Gun in order to carry out the tests. After amusing himself by firing a drum of Lewis Gun ammunition from the cupola the Chief Engineer, accompanied by the Stores Officer, returned to Corps Headquarters.'

On 26 August the Chief Engineer inspected one installed, with a variation to the gun crew accommodation, in the Amiens defence system between Blangy and Bussy, although by then the line had already moved forward following the Australian advance a few days earlier. Of the 210 sent to the Western Front from the manufacturers in Glasgow none have been found to exist today in France or Belgium.

The Canadian engineers, on inspecting the first Moir pill box in their area, at Maroeuil, gave detailed comments:

'The Moir Pill Box appears to possess certain advantages, as,
It can be quickly erected.
Affords a bullet and splinter-proof cover, and,
Can fire in all directions.
It is considered, however, that there are certain disadvantages
connected with its employment, viz.,
1. Its great weight
2. Its conspicuousness, standing as it does, three or four feet above
*   the ground.*
3. The necessity of using mass concrete for covering the dome, which
*   will require forms for placing.*
4. The fact that there is an open space of one inch all around the top
*   of the revolving curtain and the steel lip of the dome.*
5. The danger of the crew being injured by the splashing of bullets.
6. The danger of suffocation by fumes.'
(War Diary, 1st Brigade Canadian Engineers, 27th July 1918)

Other Canadians also made observations, and on the whole were enthusiastic for the design, with their Field and Tunnelling Companies constructing many over the next few months.

The American Engineers of the 30th US (Old Hickory) Division, who helped Royal Engineers to erect some around Ypres, were impressed:

'It is a very simple, effective, and unconspicuous pill-box from which
the machine gun can shoot in any direction.

The inside dimensions, six feet high by six feet in diameter, allows room for two men to work comfortably.'

(The History of the 105th Engineers)

The commander of the engineers, Colonel Joseph Hyde Pratt, made several complimentary comments on the system.

Initial British comments varied; most liked the design but some gave suggestions for improvements:

'Moir completed. This was the first we have seen. This appears to be a very excellent idea. Given material on site, 8 men can erect same in 4 days.'

(War Diary, 11th Field Company RE Company, July 1918)

'possibly of some use on back lines of defence, if well concealed, but too light and the revolving dome so easily displaced and put out of gear, that in the opinion of most M.G. officers and the writer, most machine gunners would have preferred to take their chance in the open.'

(War Diary, 560th Army Troops Company, July 1918)

Some RE units compared the practicalities of pre-cast systems such as the Moir Pill Box with in-situ concrete. One company, after visiting an early example near Aire, were not convinced:

'I consider the idea is good so far as rapid erection, after the materials are on the site, is concerned but for work in exposed positions near the front line, transport might be a difficulty owing to the weight of the blocks. The lintels weigh 300lbs each.'

(War Diary, 145 Army Troops Company RE, July 1918)

The production of noxious gasses formed when firing machine guns inside an enclosed space was a problem in most machine gun emplacements, and the small size of the Moir Pill Box exacerbated the problem. Early comments gave this as the main fault of the design:

'Assembled at Rosel first to consider the Moir Pill Box and how to counteract the tendency to poison the gun crew with the gasses from combustion of cartridges. It was stated that one or two belts in a head

wind and the crew were rendered incapable. After various discussions it was decided to ask the War Office whether they had tried cutting ventilating holes on the top of the steel canopy.'
(War Diary, Chief Royal Engineer, VI Corps, July 1918)

The problem was greatly alleviated by the design of a parabolic cup placed on the muzzle of the machine gun to propel the gasses forward and away from the enclosed space. Initial trials during the development stage were not satisfactory and more work followed. Tests at Camiers on 25 June included firing 2,400 rounds in 10 minutes with a mild headwind and a canvas door to reduce ventilation. The trial report stated:

'The persons in the "Pill Box" felt no ill effect whatsoever. Carbon monoxide test papers showed distinct blackening but this may have been due to other gasses.
It would appear that there is practically no danger from carbon monoxide poisoning when the muzzle cup is used, but care should be taken that any camouflage material does not unduly interfere with the ventilation round the moveable ring.'
(Trials Report B/527, Director of Gas Services, 26th June 1918)

The machine gunners who were to use the pill boxes made their own comments, often after their own trials. The 31st Battalion, Machine Gun Corps, considered after tests near Nieppe Wood in August, that a parabolic muzzle cup was satisfactory.

List of Entries

Formations Index

FORMATIONS INDEX

General Index